# The
# Snowshoe
# Book

## THE SNOW SHOE CALL

[Dedicated to the Montreal S.S. Club by W.G. Beers, 1874]

Here's to the slim snowshoe
In glory we renew,
Its fame will live and pleasure give
To manly hearts and true.
May its graceful dipping
The fair and brave enthral,
And with it live the echoes of
Our mountain snow shoe call.
 Tull-lul-lul-li-it-too

Chorus - Hear the wild shout of the snow shoers!

 [The call]
Ringing o'er mountain and valley!

 [The call]
Dying away in the valley.

Here's to the rousing song
We sing as we tramp along,
Over the hill it bounds and trills
In echoes clear and strong.
If the strength and glory
Of youth you would recall,
Then exercise your lungs and limbs
On snow shoes with our call.

Chorus - Hear the wild, etc.

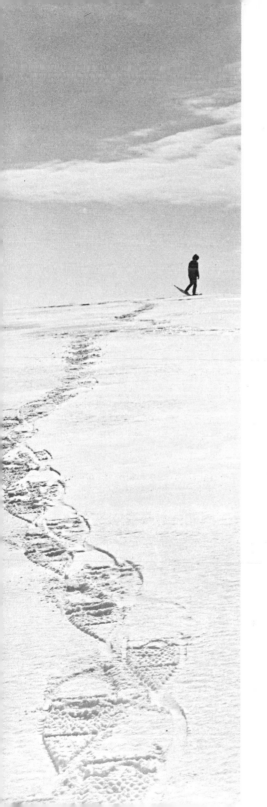

# The Snowshoe Book

## William Osgood
## and Leslie Hurley

Drawings by Grace A. Brigham

*SECOND EDITION*

The Stephen Greene Press

*Brattleboro, Vermont*

Library of Congress Cataloging in Publication Data

Osgood, William E          1926-
    The snowshoe book, second edition.

      Bibliography:    pp. 168
      1. ✓Snowshoes and snowshoeing. I. Hurley, Leslie J.,
joint author.      II.    Title.
GV853.08    1975              796.9'2            75-4769
ISBN  0-8289-0222-4
ISBN  0-8289-0221-6 pbk.

Title page photo credit:   Joel Librizzi, *Berkshire Eagle*
Tailpiece photo credit:   McCutcheon Pictorial Service

This book has been produced in the United States of
America: designed by R.L. Dothard Associates, printed
and bound by Springfield Printing Corporation. It is
published by The Stephen Greene Press, Brattleboro,
Vermont 05301.

    75  76  77  78  79  9  8  7  6  5  4  3  2  1

We dedicate our snowshoe book to all the folks who appreciate the winter scene: the solemn forests and the windswept fields. We hope that our work will appeal to those who have not yet known the pleasures of walking on the snow. We hope that our pleasures and happiness may become theirs.

# ACKNOWLEDGMENTS

For their time and patient cooperation in supplying information on snowshoe manufacture we are deeply indebted to Bastien Brothers of Village Huron, Province of Quebec, and to C. Baird Morgan, Jr., of Vermont Tubbs in Wallingford, Vermont, and for information on all aspects of snowshoeing we owe a special thanks to Roger Gilman of Middletown, Rhode Island, who lent us his extensive notes and correspondence.

For valuable general background on snowshoeing in Canada we owe much to Raoul Charbonneau of Montreal and to Mrs. Rita Starr of the Vermont Information Center in that city. Mr. Charbonneau's vast fund of knowledge about the history and activities of the Canadian Snowshoe Clubs was of immense help. More thanks are due to Yvonne and Gene Prater, whose books gave us an enlightening glimpse into snowshoe practices in the Northwest, and to Joe Delia of Skwentna, Alaska, for his insight into the special snowshoeing techniques used in the Far North.

We are also deeply indebted to James Schwedland of Dartmouth College from whom we drew material for our chapters on snowshoe selection and repair tips, and to Ronald Rood — the well known nature writer — from whose writings we gleaned much to enrich our short section on winter wild life, as well as to Bernard R. Carman of Union College and Alan French of Moor & Mountain in Concord, Massachusetts — both dedicated snowshoers — for their thoughtful reading of the manuscript.

We cannot close without a few special words of thanks to Walter E. Hard, Jr., editor of *Vermont Life* magazine, for encouragement and moral support and for good ideas at the right time, and to our friends in Northfield, Vermont, who gathered to reminisce about the Northfield Community Snowshoe Hikes, and to the many, many other people who, in one way or another, helped us to put *The Snowshoe Book* together.

William E. Osgood

Leslie J. Hurley

# Contents

6,000 Years of Snowshoeing       11

Early Beginnings, 11   Use by American Indians and Settlers, 12
Snowshoe Clubs, 16   New England Snowshoe Hikes, 21
Snowshoeing Today, 25

Selecting Snowshoes       29

Standard Styles and Their Use, 29   Unusual Variations, 36
Proper Construction, 39   The Frame, 40   The Webbing, 40
Use of Synthetics, 42   Other Check Points, 45
Weight and Size, 46   Maintenance, 46

Binding Basics       48

Simple Toe-piece and Heel Strap, 48   A Buckled Variety, 50
U.S. Army Style, 50   Flexible with Hinged Footplate, 51
Closed Toe-piece, 52   Two Native Alaskan Styles, 53
Heel Control Model, 55   Using Old Inner Tubes, 58

Clothing and Sundry       62

Footgear, 62   Underwear, 64   Outerwear, 64   Headgear, 66
For Warm Hands, 66   New Materials, 67   Costs, 68
Crampons, 69   Poles, 70   Ice Axe, 71   Extras, 71

Tips on Technique and Travel       73

First Steps, 73   Cardinal Rule, 74   Uphill Travel, 75
Edging, 77   Turning, 77   Body Movement, 78
Downhill Travel, 79   Poles as Aids, 80
Cross-Country Travel, 81   Trail Breaking, 82
Difficult Terrain, 83   Group Travel, 85
The Leader, 88   Size and Safety, 90

## Winter Safety 91

Snowshoe Repair, 92   Survival Rations, 93
First Aid Measures, 95   ABC's of Avalanches, 96
Travel Precautions, 104   Winter Rescue, 107
Self Rescue, 108   Planned Rescues, 110

## Fun for All 115

Racing, 115   Regulations, 117   Do-It-Yourself Tips, 120
Six Games, 120   Biathlon, 124

## Making Your Own 126

Getting Set, 127   Selecting the Tree, 130
Getting Out the Stock, 133   Softening the Rawhide, 138
Making the Jig, 139   Finishing the Hide, 141
The Steamer, 143   Finishing the Frames, 144
Preparing the Lacing, 147   Lacing, 148
Alternatives, 153   Emergency Snowshoes, 153

## Snowshoe Makers List 157

## For Further Reading 159

## Index 161

# The
# Snowshoe
# Book

Very old snowshoe made of branches and
bark.   *National Museum of Canada*

# 6,000 Years
# of Snowshoes

Those who have enjoyed the pleasures of slipping quietly through the snow covered forest aisles need not be reminded of the satisfactions that snowshoeing offers to all who claim an affinity with nature in winter. With this book, it is our hope to entice many new members into the ancient brotherhood of snowshoers while at the same time perhaps widening the horizons of the sport's already numerous fans.

## Early Beginnings

The use of snowshoes dates back over an incredibly long span of human history. Archeologists have been unable to date the origin of either skis or snowshoes, but the best evidence suggests that the first device to serve as a foot-extender for easier travel over the snow was originated in Central Asia about 4000 B.C. Thus the snowshoe/ski is one of the oldest inventions of man, ranking in importance with the wheel.

Without the snowshoe/ski, aboriginal peoples would not have been able to expand over, and occupy, the northern hemisphere. Once this important contribution to technology had been made, certain human groups began their northward migrations which eventually enabled them to move from a central point somewhere in Asia into what are now known as Scandinavia, Siberia and the Americas.

It is thought that Asia and the Americas were once joined by land at the place where the Bering Strait now separates the United

States from the Soviet Union. It was then that the various predecessors of the American Indian and the Eskimo moved into the Americas. This eastward migration bridge apparently became the demarcation point between the use of snowshoes and skis for there is no good evidence that skis were ever used in North America by these aboriginal peoples, except among the Aleuts. The westward moving peoples, however, evidently favored the ski for, in the course of human history, skis became the favored means of transportation in northern Asia and Europe. Interchange between Asia and the Americas in the region of the Bering Strait evidently declined and these two human populations developed independently each with its own culture. Interestingly enough the snowshoe became a major part of the North American cultural heritage.

## Indians as Innovators

Indians, as distinguished from Eskimos, were the great innovators in snowshoe design. Indians tended to move into the forested temperate zone where snowshoes were an absolute necessity for getting around in wintertime. Eskimos, living in the polar regions, did not find snowshoes essential for they traveled mostly over sea ice or on the wind-packed snow of the tundra. Accordingly, snowshoes are not too often seen amongst Eskimo groups.

The Athapascan Indians of the American and Canadian west coast and the Algonquin Indians of the Ottawa and St. Lawrence River valley areas brought the snowshoe to the greatest peak of perfection. Starting with a basic bearpaw design, they introduced hundreds of variant patterns suited to all possible conditions. Before the horse was reintroduced to America by the Spaniards, even the Plains Indians used snowshoes to hunt buffalo and it could be truly said that one common cultural characteristic of all the Indian tribes in any region where snow covered the ground in wintertime was the snowshoe.

Insofar as we know from the Norse sagas, the first white men to set foot in North America led by Leif Ericson around 1000 A.D. made no mention of snowshoes being used by the Indian groups they came upon. But there is no question that snowshoe travel was well

Indians hunting buffalo on snowshoes as depicted by George Catlin.
*Public Archives of Canada*

established at that time by Indians in Labrador and on Newfoundland. This is a curious omission in the otherwise detailed sagas.

Probably the first white people to make extensive adaptation of the snowshoe were the French who began to move in and colonize the St. Lawrence River area in the 1600's. The French tended to intermingle freely with the Indians and they quickly learned how to make best use of the snowshoe in wintertime and canoe in summer. The great heroes of the French colonial period, d'Iberville, Le Moyen, Hertel de Rouville, de Nantel and many others, were experienced snowshoers. During the prolonged French and Indian War, the struggle between French and English for dominion in North America was almost swayed to the side of the French by their superior tactics and by the way they, with their Indian allies, used snowshoes as a tactical aid for making lightning raids on English settlements.

Another Catlin painting shows an Indian war dance on snowshoes. *Public Archives of Canada*

The Dutch and English, who tended to settle further south along the Atlantic coast, were not as successful as the French in learning from the Indians. These settlers did not as quickly assimilate Indian traits. One person who did learn well from the Indians was Robert Rogers, who put his knowledge to good use as a scout for the English armies fighting on the borderlands. The famous 1758 Battle on Snowshoes near Lake George in the Adirondacks led military leaders to realize how significant snowshoes were in waging winter warfare. From that time on the English colonies, later to become the United States, made snowshoes part of their military forces' basic equipment. In the State Papers of Vermont, for example, there are several references to payments made to furnish the militia with snowshoes.

During the great westward expansion period, snowshoes were equally as important as the axe and flintlock rifle in the zones where snow lay deep throughout the winter season. Trappers, hunters,

An early Canadian soldier on snowshoes, from a 1722 French history. *Public Archives of Canada*

explorers and surveyors in these areas found snowshoes to be indispensable.

Both the Indians and the white men in these times usually made their own snowshoes according to the patterns which had been defined by the Indians long before the white men came to North America. The making of snowshoes was a home industry for the most part, although certain people who had a particular knack for the craft probably made some snowshoes for sale or barter.

Indian groups maintained the lead in snowshoe manufacture until very recent times and even now some of the best and least expensive snowshoes are made in Indian communities. A good example of this industry is the little village of Indian Lorette a short distance north of Quebec City where descendants of the Huron tribe still make an excellent product for sale in Canada and the United States (see the list of snowshoe manufacturers on page 157).

## The Spread of the Ski

Historically then, the snowshoe was dominant in North America until sometime in the 1800's when immigrating Norwegians, Swedes and Finns introduced the ski. The process of the cultural diffusion of the ski was slow at first. Indians and the white men who preceded the Scandinavians continued to prefer the snowshoe until the 1930's when skiing began to make its phenomenal rise as a major form of recreation. Even then, the form of skiing which took precedence was downhill sport, with some means of mechanical transport to get the skier to the top of the slope. Snowshoeing continued to be the principal means of utilitarian travel for trappers, hunters and woodsmen as well as for significant numbers of people who just liked to wander around in the winter forests for pure pleasure. It was not until the late 1960's that the use of skis for touring began to be popular in the United States and Canada.

## The Snowshoe Clubs

Despite the rising popularity of other forms of winter recreation, snowshoes have certainly not been displaced. This is

St. George's Snowshoe Club members pose for a formal 1884 portrait, complete with their gay uniforms and mascots. *Manitoba Archives*

especially true in Canada's Province of Quebec where the use of snowshoes is firmly rooted in tradition.

One of the particularly interesting aspects of this tradition is the snowshoe club which still has a place of honor in many parishes. The origin of these clubs apparently dates back to the time when military regiments formed teams and organized snowshoe races to whet competition and encourage physical fitness. The lineage of some of these clubs dates back more than two hundred years to early French Canadian days. Later these clubs became exclusively civilian in membership and control but a certain touch of military esprit lingered on, as was evident in their continued use of drum and bugle corps, flags and banners, officers, scouts and even mascots.

## A Bit of Dash

By far the most unique aspect of these snowshoe clubs was their tendency to create colorful uniforms with brightly colored sashes and knitted tuques. In the course of time certain colors came to be identified with particular districts. For example, blue was distinctive of the area near Montreal, white around Trois Rivieres, while red was typical of Quebec itself. Usually the color was displayed on the headgear or sashes, with the latter worn over a tunic. An arrow design often ornamented the sashes. Footgear was most often the high, soft-soled moccasin. And, of course, most important were the snowshoes which were made especially lightweight to be swift for racing.

The English in the Province of Quebec likewise were fascinated by the idea of the snowshoe club and, especially in the Montreal area, founded enthusiastic organizations with many members and interesting events. Apparently the most active of all these organizations was the Montreal Snow Shoe Club founded about 1840. In 1882 its Vice President, Hugh W. Becket, wrote a history and record of the club with a synopsis of the racing events of other clubs.

In addition to arranging racing meets, these clubs also had a strong social orientation centered on the idea of good fellowship. Often during the wintertime the members would gather of an evening and hike out to an inn or tavern where they would have a good supper and then hike back, arriving at a late hour. This idea of an evening outing drifted south into the United States as you will see in our description of the New England community snowshoe hikes. However, the strong club organization, with its races and uniforms, remained much more typical of the Canadian scene.

## Canadian Snowshoer's Union

Finally, on 9 November 1907, twenty-two clubs sent representatives to the Montreal Amateur Athletic Association to found the Canadian Snowshoer's Union which remains today as probably the largest organization of snowshoers in the world and is the prime moving force behind planning and executing races held on snowshoes. In 1964 the Union published a detailed booklet entitled *The Snowshoers Guide* which is available today and considered the bible of snowshoe racing.

Canadian snowshoe club members gather for a moonlit night outing. *Culver Pictures*

Not only does the Union oversee the management of snowshoe races, but it also seeks to maintain the historical aspects of snowshoeing and to keep alive some of the old traditions. Today a very large part of this job falls to Mr. Raoul Charbonneau at 4595 rue St. Laurent in Montreal. Mr. and Mrs. Charbonneau have spent a lifetime organizing and promoting snowshoeing in North America. In 1925 he organized the Club Laurier in Montreal and in 1936 was elected Secretary-Treasurer of the Canadian Snowshoer's Union. He also serves in the same capacity for an international club which encompasses both the United States and Canada and counts a total membership of 5,300 members of which 50 percent is made up of young people. In Canada, most of the clubs are located in the Province of Quebec with a scattering in Ontario and Manitoba. In the United States most of the clubs are in Maine, but there are also clubs in New Hampshire, Connecticut and Massachusetts.

One of Mr. Charbonneau's fond hopes is that one day the snowshoe races will be a part of the Winter Olympics. This would of course require a much more international base than snowshoeing now enjoys. If such a thing were ever to come about, it would, in large part, be due to the excellent groundwork laid by Raoul Charbonneau over the long years that he has persisted in his efforts for organized snowshoeing.

## Yankee Style

Currently, headquarters for snowshoe activity in the United States, outside of Alaska, is in Lewiston, Maine. There the Secretary of the American Snowshoe Union, Mr. Albert E. Cote of 198 Lisbon Street, oversees the Union's activities and maintains a close affiliation with the Canadian Snowshoer's Union.

And so we see that the northeastern United States and southeastern Canada have become the focal points of most organized snowshoe activity. But what about the other vast stretches of the snow covered north?

In the heavy snow belt of the northwestern United States and southwestern Canada, snowshoes are much used for mountaineering: the best information on their use in these regions is in

*Snowshoe Hikes in the Cascades and Olympics,* a wonderfully illustrated book written by Gene Prater and published by the Mountaineers (P.O. Box 122, Seattle, Washington) in 1969.

In Alaska, snowshoes are as typical as the willow ptarmigan or the dog team. The same is true of the Yukon Territory, the Atlantic Provinces and the tremendous area of the North West Territory where everywhere snowshoes are taken for granted and regarded as commonplace as air. This clearly must also be the case in many of the largely uninhabited areas of the North where snowshoes are absolutely necessary unless one owns a snowmobile and even then snowshoes often serve as an emergency link in the event of a breakdown.

## Snowshoe Hikes

In reviewing the history of snowshoeing, we cannot ignore the community snowshoe hikes which were so popular in New England villages until the late 1920's and early 30's. Reminiscences of a group in Northfield, Vermont, provide an inside look at the workings of this once very popular form of winter recreation.

Planning and organization was quite informal. At the end of any particular winter season, a group of three would take the responsibility of getting the hikes underway as soon as the snow was deep enough the following winter, usually just after the Christmas holidays. An announcement in the local newspaper invited all those who wished to assemble at a certain hour on the village square. Beforehand, the leader and his committee would have prepared a route and arranged with a farm family to give hospitality. However, information concerning the route and destination was kept secret to give a sense of novelty and suspense to the tour.

The size of these groups ranged all the way from about 30 to 100, with an average of 40 to 50 for most hikes. Old-timers and youngsters alike went along and quite often entire families turned out for the event.

In New England, snowshoers did not have special costumes for their sport. Routine outdoor clothing, chiefly heavy wool, was worn; trousers for the men and boys while the women and girls wore bloomers and sometimes skirts. A heavy mackinaw-type short coat kept the upper body warm and the headgear was a knitted tuque. Footgear was much the same then as now with high moccasins and leather-topped pacs being preferred. In Northfield the most favored style of snowshoe was the Maine model, with the Alaskan trail or pickerel snowshoe also somewhat used. Bearpaw models were apparently not much in vogue during this period. A colorful note was struck by the women who decorated their snowshoes with small tufts of red wool around the edge of the frames.

## The "Whippers-In"

After the group had gathered, the leader would strike out at a smart pace along the planned route. The main body would then fall in line, Indian file. Stationed at the end were two skilled men who bore the peculiar title of "whippers-in." It was their responsibility to see that no one was left behind. It was also their duty to assist any floundering ladies over fences or out of the deep snow and they usually carried along some scraps of leather and rawhide thongs should repairs to equipment become necessary. During the course of the march, rest stops would be made from time to time allowing the oldsters to catch their breath and the flirtatious to exchange a little flirtation.

After a couple of hours of snowshoe hiking in the brisk winter air, appetites would be whetted for the fresh-baked biscuits and homemade preserves, oyster stew, sandwiches, doughnuts, cider and coffee that would be waiting at the destination. Group singing filled the thirty or forty minutes between the arrival of the leader, and the most vigorous hikers, and that of the whippers-in. The farm family was reimbursed —10c to 25c — for the supper, depending on the situation and, no doubt, the elegance of the meal. When the hikes took place during the sugaring season it was likely that a sugar on snow party would be arranged with dill pickles and raised doughnuts to accompany the sweet maple.

## Snowshoe Sliding

After supper was finished the group would reassemble for the

Some of the Hardwick, Vermont, "Mohawks" enjoying a 1920 snowshoe outing. *From the album of Mrs. Vesta Magoon*

return trip which usually followed a different route and was planned to include, if at all possible, an open, steep, snow-covered bank down which all the hikers could slide, one snowshoe in front of the other. This part of the trip was a time for much fun and joking as some of the members tumbled head over heels down the slope when the toe of their snowshoes would catch in the snow and trip them up. Finally, the group would return to the point of departure about ten-thirty or eleven P.M. and break up for the walk to their respective homes and a good night's sleep.

Sometime during the course of each snowshoe hike, arrangements would be made for a committee to plan the next hike, and these people would have the responsibility of keeping the continuity so that, if conditions were right, snowshoe enthusiasts could count on weekly hikes throughout the winter.

While these community snowshoe hikes have not disappeared altogether, their popularity has been largely eroded by the multiplicity of evening activities which take up our time these days; this, plus the fact that the popularity of downhill skiing has drawn the attention of the younger members of the community snowshoe clubs away from this tradition. But that too is changing!

## New England Family Outing

Another type of outing very popular in New England was the family weekend breakfast hike. Especially planned so that the youngsters could tag along on their tiny snowshoes, a typical outing of this sort took place in two parts. The first stage encompassed a late Saturday hike either by moonlight or lantern light out to a dense stand of huge white pine trees where a roaring campfire would be built and a kettle of water hung to boil over the flames. Oatmeal was then stirred into the water and, after the mixture began to cook, the kettle transferred into what was known in those days as a "fireless cooker." This cooker was nothing more than a tight box insulated with sawdust or hay, with its purpose, of course, to preserve the heat so that slow cooking could continue all through the night.

Once this important task was accomplished, the embers of the campfire would be carefully banked to be in readiness for the next morning. After a last look around the campsite, the family would snowshoe back to the house — a trip of usually less than a mile, but seeming much longer to the young folks who had been made drowsy by the lateness of the hour and the flickering flames.

On Sunday morning everyone would be up early in anticipation of the outdoor breakfast and load a toboggan with eating utensils, a huge black iron frying pan, an enameled coffee pot equipped with a bail and hook so it could be hung over the fire, and the necessary bacon, sausages and eggs. With all these the family would set out again, this time over a well-packed snowshoe trail, with everyone pulling on the long rope to drag the heavily laden toboggan up the hills and across the fields. On the downgrades one person would transfer to the rear to pick up the trailing rope and hold back the toboggan from going too fast.

At the campsite the ashes would be drawn away from the coals still glowing with sufficient heat to fry the sausages, eggs and bacon. While a separate, small fire of dry pinewood was kindled to boil water for coffee, the "fireless cooker" was opened and generous servings of steaming oatmeal porridge ladled out for one and all. Usually this was eaten with thick cream and honey and, when combined with fried eggs, sausages and bacon and good coffee, made a breakfast intended to stick to your ribs. After breakfast all the eating and cooking utensils were loaded back on the toboggan for washing up later at the house.

After such a breakfast one had to do something to work it off, so the various family members would work in the pine grove trimming dead branches off the trees and carrying them by the armload back to the campsite for future fires. All of this work was done on snowshoes and was excellent practice for the young folks whose contribution in armloads of pine branches, though slight, nevertheless gave them a good sense of participation in a family effort plus the experience of walking on snowshoes while balancing a load.

With minor variations, little weekend excursions like this were a commonplace activity in many New England families. They certainly remain as vivid memories in the minds of the young participants and serve as an incentive to continue the tradition in succeeding generations. And a splendid tradition at that.

## Snowshoeing Today

By far the greatest use of snowshoes today is for recreation — purely and simply to get into sympathetic oneness with the winter landscape. Man is often made anew by such a simple activity as snowshoeing — truly recreation in the finest sense of the word. Such an experience may revitalize the human spirit, often jaded by the raucous clamor of urban life and insistent demands of a complex civilization. For, as the mind and body relax, a welcome serenity quietly replaces the strained and brittle patchwork of today's conflict and disorder. If there were only an accurate measure of these satisfactions, snowshoeing would likely outrank the most potent tranquilizer and thoughtful doctors might prescribe snowshoes in place of elaborate and costly laboratory compounds.

Just as snowshoeing rewards the mind and spirit it also rewards the body, firming up muscles that often don't get enough of a work-

out in our rather sedentary world. At the same time it has the advantage of not being *too* demanding. Snowshoeing is a sport of
moderation so far as energy expenditure is concerned. Only slightly
more effort is needed to get around on snowshoes than to walk on
dry ground. Of course it is possible to put heavy demands on the
body when using snowshoes for mountaineering or in racing but, for
most people, snowshoeing is a sport they can enjoy all their lives in a
quiet, undramatic — yet rewarding — way.

## Other Ends

Even though a large number of people use snowshoe travel as
an end in itself, many others use snowshoes as a means to further
some other end. One rather common use is for winter hunting and
trapping. In the deep snow belt snowshoes are an indispensable aid
to tending a trap line or for getting into position for a shot at a hare
flashing across a clearing. Hares themselves have evolved hind feet
similar in form and function to the snowshoe which enable them to
travel easily over deep snow. So it's fair to say that, more often than
not, all concerned — the hunter and the hunted — use snowshoes
(except the poor hounds who have to struggle through the deep snow
as best they can).

Another large group in the roster of snowshoers is made up of
such people as timber cruisers, foresters, surveyors, prospectors,
land speculators and electric power and telephone linemen. These
people see snowshoes as primarily utilitarian implements, important
in the day-to-day performance of their duties.

## The Snowmobile

The most recent history of the snowshoe must have some
reference to the incredibly rapid rise in the popularity of the
snowmobile. In looking at this phenomenon, one surely wonders if
snowmobiles will completely displace the snowshoe. To some extent
this has happened. However, despite the skyrocketing snowmobile sales, snowshoe manufacturers report that they have never
had it so good. In the summer of 1970, one leading snowshoe

Present-day snowshoe group catching their breath after a vigorous assault of Pine Mountain near Gorham, New Hampshire.   *Photo by Dick Smith*

maker reported that he was six months behind on orders and this was not an isolated instance. Perhaps some of this is accounted for by the fact that many snowmobilers carry snowshoes with them in order to penetrate dense thickets or to provide emergency transport.

Of the people who care about winter recreation there seem to be four distinct categories: downhill skiers, snowmobilers, cross-country skiers and snowshoers. The last two categories have a close affinity. Snowshoers and cross-country skiers tend to scorn the snowmobile as an effete, rackety nuisance. At best there is an uneasy alliance between the two groups of people. The snowmobilers on the one hand tend to have a more close-knit form of organization. They are definitely group-minded; whereas the cross-country skiers and the snowshoers are more individualistic. One could go on at some length to analyze this curious set of differences, but this is not our intention.

Suffice it to say now that the snowshoe, almost six thousand years old, is holding its own in this incredibly complex technological age. Undoubtedly there is something in its simplicity and its closeness with nature that speaks directly to an increasing group of people who seek now to live with nature, not to subdue it.

# Selecting Snowshoes

## Snowshoe Styles

Over the millenia a tremendous variety of snowshoe models have evolved, perhaps numbering in the hundreds. An inventory of all the recorded styles would be an intriguing study in itself, but here we will restrict ourselves to those that are commonly available, although at the same time touching upon some of the interesting variations.

## For Heavy Woods and Frequent Turning . . .

Our experience leads us to suggest that the oval-shaped *bearpaw* snowshoe with some refinements in design is the most universally satisfactory model. The basic bearpaw style functions most effectively in heavily wooded country or in situations where making frequent turns are necessary. However, the basic style does have a few handicaps and snowshoe makers have altered its design in two different ways which have improved it considerably.

One improved model is most frequently referred to as the *otter* or *Green Mountain modified bearpaw*. While still retaining the rounded tail of the standard bearpaw, it is narrower and longer and has some up-turn added to the front. The second improved model, commonly called the *Westover modified bear paw*, retains the basic oval shape of the bearpaw, but a stubby, squared-off tail has been substituted for the rounded tail of the standard bearpaw.

29

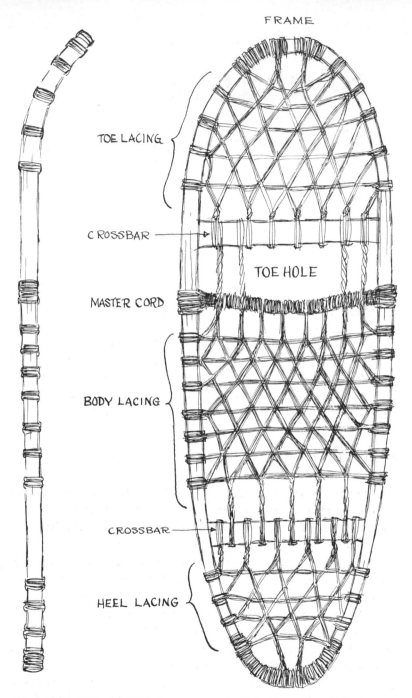

FRAME

TOE LACING

CROSSBAR

TOE HOLE

MASTER CORD

BODY LACING

CROSSBAR

HEEL LACING

Green Mountain modified bearpaw, one of the most popular snowshoe models.

## For Hilly Going . . .

In making a choice between the two improved models keep in mind the fact that the so-called Green Mountain or otter bearpaw is probably best for hilly and mountainous country where its narrow shape makes it less inclined to tilt downslope. Over more moderate terrain the Westover style bearpaw might have a slight advantage in that it would have less tail drag and thus require less effort. With us, and from all the information we have been able to gather, it's pretty much a toss-up between these two models of the improved bearpaw. Both are very good and are a substantial improvement over the standard bearpaw design.

## For Trails and Open Areas . . .

In our estimation, the next most useful snowshoe style is the one used for both the *Michigan* and *Maine* models. These two models are practically synonymous; they both offer a teardrop shape with a broad and slightly upturned nose and a long and narrow tail. Probably, if one were asked to sketch a snowshoe from memory, this is the style which would appear on paper. It is a classic design, especially in the Northeast. We have also seen it described as the *Algonquin* snowshoe.

For those who wish to be meticulous about distinguishing between the Maine and Michigan styles, the Maine style has a more pointed nose with slightly more upturn while the Michigan model has a rounded nose with slightly less upturn. Either of these models are good for traveling along trails or in open wooded areas. Their long tails make them track in a straight line with the way the feet are pointed. Beyond that, when the bindings are properly mounted on either the Maine or Michigan snowshoes, they are tail-heavy which is not only an advantage in keeping them on course, as noted above, but is helpful in bringing the tips up out of deep snow.

The current United States and Canadian military snowshoes have been patterned after the Maine model snowshoe. No doubt the procurement agencies have made a long study of the effectiveness of

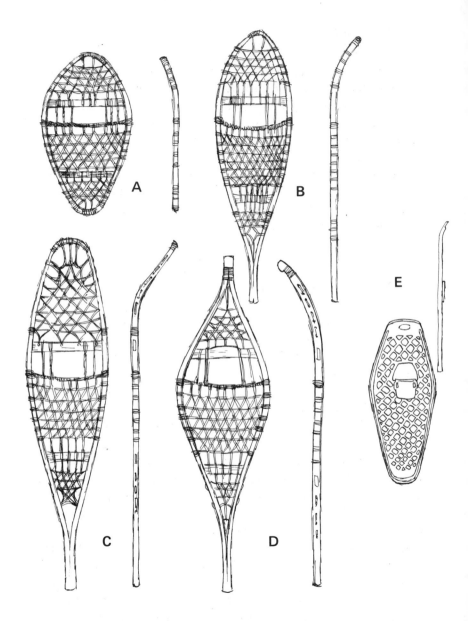

Top and side views of five snowshoe models. A is the standard bearpaw; B, the Maine or Michigan; C, the Alaskan; D, the Ojibwa; and E, a new plastic model.

each style so this should be a vote of confidence for the Maine-Michigan design. We ourselves have probably used this design more extensively than any other and have been perfectly satisfied with it, even though our bias still runs slightly in favor of the modified bearpaw models.

## For Deep Snow . . .

Another popular snowshoe style now generally available is the *Alaskan,* sometimes called the *Trail, Yukon or pickerel* snowshoe. This model is quite different in appearance from those we have discussed thus far, being particularly long and narrow, and having a most distinctively upturned toe. These snowshoes are exceptionally fine for travel in deep snow and open country. They have very little tendency to tip sidewise (which is one of the handicaps of the standard bearpaw model) and the upward flair at the toe makes it next to impossible to catch the tips in deep snow or under a crust. Heavy persons will find that the Alaskan snowshoe is best for them as its long length tends to give more support and stability. In situations requiring many short turns, this length is a decided disadvantage; likewise, in thick brush and in heavily wooded areas, the Alaskan model snowshoe is cumbersome, but for making time on the trail this snowshoe is unexcelled. This model is quite widely available in Canada and the United States through leading sports stores and mail order houses, as are the other frequently seen snowshoe models mentioned above.

Another snowshoe style to consider is the *Ojibwa.* Although we have had no personal experience with this style and it is not frequently seen in the United States, it is available here. The style of the Ojibwa is very similar to the Alaskan, and, we understand, best used in open country and deep snow. Like the Alaskan, it is long and narrow with a strong upturn at the tip. However, instead of being rounded at the tip, the tip of the Ojibwa is pointed — the result of its frame being made of two pieces of wood joined at tip and tail. One advantage to this type of construction is to avoid having to make the wide bend at the tip which requires special steaming techniques. Also there is an inherent advantage in a pointed tip as far as snowshoeing technique is concerned: the tip knifes through deep snow and does not load up. These snowshoes are available from several of the Canadian manufacturers (see list in the back of the book) and from at least one of the major camping and sporting goods suppliers here in the United States.

## A Plastic Newcomer

The snowshoe styles we have discussed so far are all wood framed with lacing of either rawhide or Neoprene. Nowadays, in addition to these now standard styles, there are snowshoe models which actively reflect modern technology. Perhaps the one style that has had the most immediate acceptance is the plastic snowshoe made of polypropylene and cast as one unit (including a hinge which is part of the binding). These snowshoes have the trade name *"Snowtreads,"* and have wide distribution through retail outlets in the United States as well as listings in the catalogs of several mail order houses. In shape, Snowtreads resemble a modified bearpaw style.

We have had some limited experience with them and find them strong enough, although we do feel that the bindings are awkward. Some of our correspondents report that they have cut the plastic hinge off entirely and have attached a standard leather or Neoprene binding in its place and find this arrangement to be a great improvement. Other people report that Snowtreads tend to tilt sideways in deep snow (this drawback was mentioned earlier as a disadvantage of the bearpaw model) and they also report that the short tail tends to kick up snow against the back of the leg (this too a drawback of the standard bearpaw model).

The great advantage of these plastic snowshoes is their comparatively low price — in the fifteen to twenty dollar range in the United States, along with the fact that they need practically no maintenance and are so easy to carry. Perhaps the best use for such snowshoes is as emergency equipment on snowmobiles and for people who need snowshoes for short trips from time to time, but do not plan to walk long distances often. Esthetically, they are displeasing, being a creature of the Plastic Age, and thus representing one of the less agreeable aspects of our time.

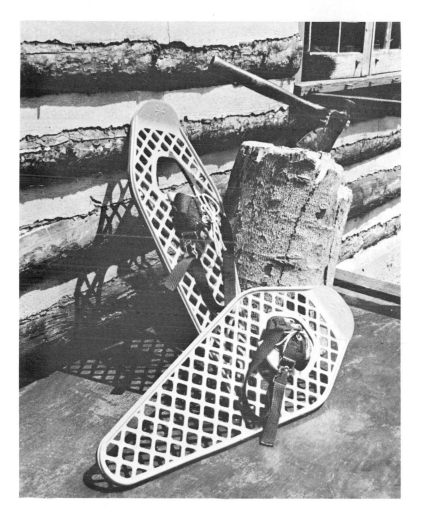

A lightweight and economical plastic version of the standard bearpaw snowshoe. *Eastman Kodak photo*

## Ideal for Backpacking

Another innovation in snowshoe manufacture is a style made with a tubular aluminum frame, wooden crossbars and lacing in the foot section which has been punched out of rawhide and lashed to the frame. In shape, they are similar to the Green Mountain bearpaw, being rather narrow and with rounded tips and tails. They appear to be rather flimsy and look as though they would fold up under heavy use. However, a respected fellow snowshoer, Roger Gilman, gave these snowshoes extensive use in the winter of 1970-71 and reports that they were very satisfactory.

These aluminum-frame snowshoes are available from several sources — Black Forest Enterprises of Nevada City, California, for one, and the Sher-Craft Company of Sherbrooke, P.Q., for another (see list of snowshoe manufacturers at back of book).

Of all the snowshoes we have seen, except perhaps the very light racing models, this style is the lightest. This factor, coupled with their durability, make these aluminum and rawhide snowshoes an ideal choice for backpacking on trips where snowshoes may only be used periodically. Their toughness and durability seems to have been well documented by experienced snowshoers. They might well be the first choice for rescue units, telephone and electric linemen and others who need snowshoes from time to time. This type of snowshoe is especially advertised as emergency equipment for snowmobilers and at least one snowmobile manufacturer we know of distributes these snowshoes in three sizes.

Another style made of magnesium has been developed by the United States and Canadian military services. Ultra light weight, it has a welded construction and webbing of nylon covered aircraft control cable. Though billed as outlasting regular style snowshoes seven times, this model is quite expensive.

## Variations on the Theme

As we have seen, there are commonly available a number of standard styles of snowshoes from which to choose according to your particular needs. Here, however, we would like to detail some of the interesting variations in style that have been developed for special (extraordinary) purposes over the years.

For example, what about snowshoes for horses? In an interesting woodcut dating from 1555, Olaus Magnus, the historian of the North, shows a man leading a pack horse with both leader and horse shod in peculiar round snowshoes. This is exceptional, not only for the fact that the illustration shows snowshoes on a horse, but also because it indicates that a form of snowshoe was being used in

Sixteenth century woodcut shows a mountaineer and his pack horse both shod in unusual round snowshoes. *Culver Pictures*

Scandinavia during the sixteenth century where, currently, snowshoes are seldom used. Our Alaskan correspondent, Joe Delia of Skwentna, also notes that horses have been trained to walk on round snowshoes for work near the mines in Alaska. Perhaps the idea for these round snowshoes for horses came from observing how well the round hooves of the caribou and reindeer adapt to travel in the snow.

The most unusual homemade snowshoes we have ever seen came from New England where Wendell H. Savery of Williamstown, Vermont, showed us one made entirely of wood. Now, snowshoes made entirely of wooden boards are not too uncommon; we have seen several examples of these. The peculiar feature of Mr. Savery's snowshoe was that a third crossbar had been added to the conventional teardrop frame. This additional crossbar was set well forward and made to pivot by two pins set into holes bored through the frame. A large wooden footrest was firmly attached to this movable front crossbar. This footrest was designed to come down on the other two crossbars which were mortised into the frame in the usual way, using them as a platform. A second distinctive feature was the lack of any webbing at all.

Unusual, and rather uncomfortable looking, wooden snowshoes owned by W.H. Savery of Williamstown, Vermont.

Our readers may wonder how snowshoes made entirely of wood differ from skis. In the first place, the examples of wooden snowshoes we have seen are perfectly flat and so, if slid forward, would dig into the snow instead of skimming on or near the surface. Secondly, these wooden snowshoes had cleats nailed crosswise on the bottom for reinforcement. These cleats would certainly prevent them from sliding as skis are intended to do. Some of these wooden snowshoes have toe holes cut through the wood, while others are solid. The latter must have been quite awkward to use because the toe hole is a distinct improvement for easy travel.

While we are on the subject of "near-skis" we should mention the combination designed in Switzerland and made by Lillywhites, Ltd., of Great Britain. This is a small snowshoe, not much larger than foot-size, laced with string and mounted directly on a short, broad ski. Apparently this hybrid never became popular for, as we mentioned earlier, Roger Gilman, our correspondent in Switzerland, reports that snowshoes are still a curiosity there.

The Aleuts of the Alaska Peninsula have a device for over-snow travel which is basically a ski in form and design. The frame is about ten inches wide by five feet long and is entirely covered with sealskin with the hair pointing backward. Such a snowshoe/ski would be slid along the surface of the snow and one would be prevented from slipping backwards by the slope of the hair. This, of course, is the same principle long used by skiers who attach special climbing skins to the underside of their skis for extended climbs. Joe Delia, who mentioned the Aleutian snowshoe/ski in one of his letters, said he had never seen an example of them, only heard about them from older natives.

There is now on the market a short, stubby "Bushwhacker" ski made on the principle invented ages ago by the Aleuts. It is distributed in the U.S. by Trak of Newburyport, Massachusetts at about sixty dollars for the skis and bindings. However, instead of using a sealskin bottom, a plastic base is applied and imprinted with a fishscale pattern which allows the "Bushwhacker" to slide forward and prevents it from slipping backward. We have tried these skis and find them excellent, having the best qualities of both snowshoes and skis.

Also from Alaska comes news of some enormous snowshoes appropriately called "whales." These are fourteen inches wide by *seven* feet long. Joe Delia says that these monsters are absolutely essential for traveling over the heavy snows found on the southern slopes of the Alaska Range.

Another snowshoe variation designed for use in the deep, light snows of Canada is sometimes referred to as the "beavertail." The most common dimension for this style is nineteen by twenty-six inches. It is the most nearly circular of all the snowshoes we have seen except the exotic specimens recorded by Olaus Magnus. The "beavertail" is usually laced with a very fine mesh to give maximum support in soft snow.

To round out our list of off-the-beaten-track snowshoes — Swedish manufacturers now have for sale a saucer-shaped snowshoe which is short and wide. The frame, curiously enough, is made of bamboo. The lacing is provided from wide straps of rubber or Neoprene impregnated canvas. The style is apparently derived from the Norwegian "Truger," a snowshoe for emergency use and not much good for long distance travel because there is no toe hole.

## Snowshoe Construction

The proper construction of snowshoes is not only an interesting study but an important thing to know when one is planning to acquire a new pair of snowshoes. The following look at the steps

involved in this years-old craft will give our readers an idea of what
to look for.

## The Frame

White ash is the best wood for snowshoe frames. It should be
selected for slow growth and straight grain and should preferably be
air-dried rather than kiln-dried. The air-dried wood has longer life.
Nowadays, most of the frame stock is quarter-sawn, but the very best
frame stock has been split from the tree in such a way that the grain
is only slightly interrupted thus giving incredible strength. Only a
few hand craftsmen will take the time to split out frame stock so
your chances of finding this kind of material are very slight.
Quarter-sawn frame stock makes up the bulk of what is used for
commercially manufactured snowshoes. Look the frame over
carefully and examine the grain of the wood to be sure that it runs
straight and that there are no knots or other visible defects.

Also considered as part of the frame are the wooden crossbars,
usually two in number. Examine the joints where the crossbars are
mortised into the frame and be sure that the workmanship there is
neat and tight. The edges of the crossbars and frame should be
rounded to eliminate sharpness and to give a clean, smooth appearance. Holes bored through the frame and crossbars should be
slightly countersunk to eliminate sharp edges that might wear into
the webbing. If you are selecting snowshoes with metal frames be
sure that all bends are smooth, that there are no crimps and, if the
style of frame involves a joining of the ends of the frame, look over
the workmanship of this joint carefully and reject any frames with
ill-made joints whether welded or otherwise fastened.

## The Webbing

No matter what the material used for lacing snowshoes, whether
synthetic or natural, the most important point to consider is the
tightness of the strands. Loose or slack webbing indicates poor
workmanship and, especially in snowshoes laced with rawhide, the

Trained Vermont craftsman in early stages of "filling" snowshoe webbing. *Stephen T. Whitney photo*

slackness will increase as the snowshoes get wet. Walking on snowshoes with slack webbing is rather like walking on a soggy pancake fried in lukewarm grease — an awful sensation!

The webbing, netting, filling or lacing of snowshoes is an interesting story in itself. The basic concept behind snowshoe lacing is to provide enough light, yet strong and durable, surface area to keep a person from sinking down too deeply into the snow. In addition, the lacing should be attached to the snowshoe frame in such a way as not to weaken the frame unnecessarily. Since snow comes in a multitude of forms, varying from one part of the winter to another and also in one part of the snow belt to another, one will find that the basic snowshoe designs have been refined to suit various conditions and geographical regions. Perhaps the most elaborate refinements have been in the various types of webbing or filling. For coarse, granular surfaces, sometimes called "corn" snow, or thick crusts and wind-packed surfaces, a heavy, open webbing is best. On the other hand, a fine mesh is desirable for travel in light, fluffy snows.

For most snowshoes, there are three sections to be considered as far as lacing is concerned. The first and most important section is the center — usually between the front and rear crossbars. Here is where the foot is attached and where the main weight distribution falls. Generally the materials used to lace this section are heavier and the weave more open. In some cases, though rarely, this is the only section to be filled and the front (toe) and rear (heel) sections are left open. Usually, however, the front and rear sections are filled, commonly with a lighter gauge material than that used for the main or center section. The method of attachment to the frame is different also. In most cases the lacing is attached to the center section by wrapping while, for the front and rear sections, holes are often bored through the frame to provide attachment points.

## Synthetics on Trial

What of the materials used for snowshoe webbings? Today almost all agree that synthetics make the best webbing. The specific synthetics in this case are a combination of nylon fabric and a heavy Neoprene coating. This form of webbing is resistant to most forms of

Three members of the Teslin Indian Band — George Sidney, Mrs. Lena Sidney and Allison Jackson — manufacturing snowshoes at home in the Yukon. George is bending and shaping while Allison and Lena are adding the webbing. *Courtesy of Reverend J.P. Tanquay*

decay, is not attractive to gnawing animals, is water repellent and is tremendously strong. An important added feature is the fact that it does not tend to stretch when moist so that, if the snowshoes are well made and laced tightly to begin with, they will stay that way indefinitely. Another attractive feature is the fact that snow does not cling to the Neoprene coating meaning that snowshoes laced with synthetics do not load up with snow as quickly as those laced with natural materials.

Although this is still the subject of some discussion, most indications point to the fact that Neoprene coated lacings will last as long or longer than rawhide. As a matter of fact, the well-known snowshoe maker, Clarence Iverson of Shingleton, Michigan says, "We find the Neoprene we use in our shoes lasts about four times longer than the rawhide lace."

*Rawhide, Tried and True*

Rawhide, until recently, has provided most of the webbing for snowshoes. Simply defined, rawhide is the skin of some animal with the hair removed. Such a skin is not tanned in the usual sense, but first dried for preservation, then soaked in water so it can be cut into strips and made flexible for the lacing process. The rawhide shrinks in drying after the lacing is done so that a well-laced pair of snowshoes has taut webbing. Next the snowshoes are usually treated with a waterproof varnish to keep moisture from getting at the rawhide and loosening it up.

Our investigations reveal that the very best natural material for snowshoe lacing is beaver hide, but since beaver skins are more valuable with the fur on, it is a rare pair of snowshoes that is laced with beaver hide. Next in line for snowshoe webbing is ordinary cowhide taken from two-year-old steers. Caribou and reindeer hides have also been used extensively. However, these skins are not as good as cowhide because they tend to stretch more easily. Moosehides, sealskins and bearskins have also been noted as useful for snowshoe webbing.

It may be interesting to note that these various hides when used for snowshoe lacing fall under the term *babiche* (sometimes, babbiche or bacbiche) — undoubtedly an Indian name which has been used enough by English speaking people to be generally understood in backwoods sections. We have heard snowshoe lacings referred to as "gut," but have never known of any which were actually laced with gut which, strictly speaking, would be made from the intestines of some animal rather than from its hide.

Although animal hides make up by far the bulk of natural materials used in lacing snowshoes, there are some instances where vegetable products have been used. From Yugoslavia and Czechoslovakia we have heard of shrubs being cut and trimmed for snowshoe webbing, being woven in a wickerwork fashion. And, in North America, we know of many instances where twigs and stems of bushes have been used to good advantage to get out of a tight spot.

*Patterns*

Lacing patterns generally are designed to give a woven

hexagonal effect in the front, center and rear sections, but hexagonal webbing is by no means universal. In Alaska it is quite common to see a rectangular lacing pattern in the center section while the front and rear sections may be laced with a hexagonal network. Interesting variations in weaving snowshoe lacings may be seen from time to time, especially in Canada, and some of these are real collectors' items as the pattern designs are often quite complex and artistic.

Recently another process has been developed for making snowshoe webbing. This process eliminates the time consuming and expensive weaving process of filling the lacing in snowshoes. The new process consists of taking a piece of rawhide and punching holes in it with a special die. The punched rawhide is then trimmed to fit the inside of the frame, a toe hole is cut and the whole lacing is lashed to the frame with rawhide thongs, with extra reinforcement at the toe or master cord to which the binding is attached. After the rawhide is attached the whole snowshoe is treated with epoxy resin to make it waterproof. The only snowshoes we have seen using this new method of construction are the aluminum-framed snowshoes made by the Canadian Lacrosse Company, and others, mentioned earlier.

Japanese-made snowshoes laced with nylon cord have recently been seen on the market and we have also seen a number of homemade snowshoes laced with the halyard weave nylon. Snowshoes properly laced taut with nylon cord do not stretch and sag in service. Nylon is a good substitute for rawhide and certainly easier to obtain.

As noted, the magnesium-frame snowshoe developed by the United States and Canada uses nylon covered metal cable for the lacing. This cable is of 1/32" diameter for the front and rear sections and 1/16" diameter for the center section. However, these too have been untested by us.

## Other Important Points

Be sure to check the master cord (sometimes called the toe cord). This is the heavy cord running straight across the snowshoe just below the toe hole to which bindings are attached. The master cord takes the most punishment of any part of the snowshoe so, accordingly, it should have the most attention in construction.

Another important point to consider is the size of the toe hole. When bindings are properly mounted, the ball of the foot should be just about over the master cord. This means that the front of the boot should be able to move in and out of the toe hole without rubbing on the sides or on the front crossbar. A large toe hole is especially needed by those who intend to wear heavy insulated rubber boots.

Weight is another very important consideration to keep in mind when selecting a pair of snowshoes. Our chart (see opposite) suggests the proper snowshoe dimensions for persons of different weights. Don't choose the biggest snowshoes under the impression that they will keep you on the surface no matter what the consistency of the snow. Aim for the lightest weight possible for anything and everything to be attached to your feet — whether it be snowshoes, socks, boots, or bindings. Keep in mind that one pound on your feet is the equivalent of five pounds on your back. There is nothing to be gained in walking around with heavy, awkward snowshoes. Choose the lightest and trimmest you can find. Your reward will be miles of pleasant excursions and a pleasant feeling of exertion at the end of a journey instead of dull exhaustion.

## Maintenance

Wood frame snowshoes with rawhide lacing should be given a coat of waterproof spar varnish whenever the finish gets worn. This will help keep the rawhide from soaking up water and loosening up. Synthetic lacing (nylon/Neoprene) does not need to be varnished but it is a good idea to varnish the wooden frames from time to time. When not in use snowshoes should be stored in a cool, dry place and hung out of the reach of gnawing animals, particularly in the case of snowshoes laced with rawhide (rodents don't seem to care much for Neoprene).

## SNOWSHOE SIZE GUIDE

| weight (in pounds) | size (in inches) |
|---|---|

Bearpaw - modified (the "Westover" style)

| 125 — 150 | 12 x 34 |
| 150 — 180 | 13 x 35 |
| 180 — 210 | 14 x 35 |

Bearpaw - modified (the "Green Mountain" style)

| up to 200 | 10 x 36 |

Bearpaw - standard

| 150 — 175 | 14 x 30 |
| 175 — 200 | 15 x 30 |
| 175 — 200 | 13 x 33 |
| 200 — 250 | 14 x 36 |

Maine

| 35 — 50 | 9 x 30 |
| 50 — 60 | 10 x 36 |
| 60 — 90 | 11 x 40 |
| 100 — 125 | 12 x 42 |
| 125 — 150 | 12 x 48 |
| 150 — 175 | 13 x 48 |
| 175 — 200 | 14 x 48 |

Michigan

| 150 — 175 | 13 x 48 |
| 175 — 200 | 14 x 48 |
| 200 — 250 | 14 x 52 |

Alaskan

| 125 — 150 | 10 x 48 |
| 150 — 175 | 10 x 56 |
| 175 — 200 | 12 x 60 |

# Binding Basics

There seems to be no doubt that bindings — or what holds the feet to the snowshoes — are the most controversial part of the whole apparatus of snowshoeing. One reason for this is that a binding that seems to be practical and dependable for one sort of terrain turns out to be difficult on another. There are two ways to lick this problem. The first, and most expensive way is to pick out one pair of snowshoes and bindings for mountaineering and another set for traveling over moderate terrain. The second possibility is to have one pair of snowshoes and several sets of interchangeable bindings, each to be used for the conditions to which they are best suited. The first alternative of course requires the greater investment.

We have tried a whole range of snowshoe bindings and will share our experience here. However, any advice offered is far from the last word and we would be glad to hear from any of our readers from their own fund of knowledge so that we can further improve this section in any editions to come.

## A Simple Combination

The most usual binding in the northeastern United States and eastern Canada is a simple combination of wide toe-piece and leather heel strap with a cross strap over the instep (see diagram A). The advantage of this uncomplicated binding is its cheapness and ease of manufacture. With a supply of good leather, a sharp knife and a punch almost anyone could make up a set of these bindings in

Three versions of an *all purpose binding*. At top, A, a common commercial style. Below, a two-step diagram shows how to put together a homemade version with a piece of leather and a bit of nylon strapping. B, at right, is a simple buckled variety.

A

LEATHER TOE PIECE

NYLON STRAPPING

B

WIDE TOE PIECE
LEATHER HEEL STRAP
CROSS STRAP OVER INSTEP

an evening's time. The wide toe-piece is cut so it is narrower in the front than in the back, thus shaped to fit the toe. On flat country and on gentle slopes this binding serves the purpose, but in climbing steep grades and in traversing hillsides this binding shows its weak points. The leather tends to stretch under tension so that your foot will sometimes slip out, or, in the case of making long traverses, your heel will slew downslope at an angle to the line of travel making it extremely difficult to walk comfortably.

This binding as it is commercially made (diagram B) usually has a buckle fitted to the heel strap and should be adjusted so the buckle is on the outside just below the ankle bone. The buckles can be dispensed with in a homemade pair. The ends should be long enough so they can be crossed behind the heel and tied at the instep at the point where one would tie the laces on a pair of oxford shoes. In former times, lamp wicking was often used for this heel strap and it must be admitted that lamp wicking is easier to tie than leather. However, lamp wicking tends to freeze up and, of course, nowadays is scarcely available at all. A good substitute for lamp wicking is nylon strapping about 1/2" or 5/8" wide. We have had good success with a combination of this nylon strapping and a leather toe piece and, as we mentioned previously, this makes a very inexpensive type of binding good for most purposes except mountaineering.

## An Army Variation

A variation on this conventional style of binding was developed by the U.S. Army and came into civilian use through surplus sales. This binding (diagram C) is a combination of leather and metal. A leather toe piece similar to that described above is attached to a metal plate which serves as a foot rest. A hinge pin passes through this plate at its fore-edge just above the master (or toe) cord. The pin is secured at either end by metal straps which are bound in position by the rawhide at each side of the toe hole. The metal straps also are bent around the front crossbar so that the whole assembly becomes an integral part of the snowshoe itself. A further refinement is the addition of crust spikes or crampons located alongside the toe hole in line with the master cord. Some users have remarked that these crust spikes are a nuisance and advise that they be cut off while

Top and bottom views of the U.S. *Army snowshoe binding*, with the metal plate and leather toe-piece shown clearly from above and the crust spikes from below. This binding was designed by Jack Burgess of Wallingford, Vermont.

others find the crust spikes quite helpful. Our experience indicates that they are worth keeping, although they may need some supplementary aids on hard crust. The remaining parts of this Army binding are conventional; being heel and instep straps as described above. (The U.S. Army binding is available from the Snocraft Company of Saco, Maine.)

This Army snowshoe binding can be improved by attaching the Army flexible ski binding to the hinged metal foot plate (diagram D). The basic element in this flexible ski binding is a strip of very heavy balata-treated canvas. An integral part of the canvas strip is a leather heel cup with strap to tighten across the instep. Also included with the flexible ski binding is a double-strapped leather toe-piece. This toe-piece has holes punched in it to match one of several sets of holes punched in the balata canvas. This choice of holes allows the length of the canvas to be extended to fit several sizes of boots just by choosing the correct set of holes. The flexible ski binding was designed to be attached to skis with wood screws, but where the ski binding is used in combination with the hinged metal plate of the standard Army snowshoe binding, the attachment is

Two views of the *Army flexible ski binding* adapted for snowshoeing. The view at right shows the adjustable canvas footplate.

balata-treated canvas

D

made with copper rivets rather than with wood screws. By using the flexible ski binding in combination with the standard snowshoe binding, one obtains much better lateral control of the snowshoe without sacrificing the freedom of vertical movement afforded by the hinged metal plate. The disadvantage, of course, lies in the added weight factor because the flexible ski binding weighs slightly more than the leather harness that is routine on the regular Army snowshoe binding. However, for those who like to tinker, we believe this modification is worth the effort.

Another type of binding very similar to the standard combination of wide toe-piece and leather heel strap is one on which the toe-piece folds back over the toe of the boot (diagram E). That is, the toe-piece of the binding is not open at both ends, but only at the rear where the boot can be inserted. This flap of leather or Neoprene is held in place over the toe of the boot by two straps with a buckle for adjustment. The straps also serve to attach the toe-piece to the master cord. The main advantage of this modified harness is that the boot is held from slipping forward which is certainly a great help in going downhill.

In the *forward support binding*, a wide leather piece keeps the toe from sliding forward, a very helpful improvement, especially for downhill travel. It also protects the toes when digging in for a steep climb.

E

## Alaskan Favorites

When we first thought about writing this book we wrote to as many people as possible to find out about different styles of snowshoes and bindings. One of our most informative replies came from Joe Delia, an Alaskan trapper from Skwentna, and in his letter he carefully described a most unique form of snowshoe binding. This binding (diagram F) was originally devised by Alaskan natives and has a long history there. It consists of a toe strap much narrower than the one described above. The heel straps are riveted or sewn to the toe strap in such a way that they fit at the sides of the boots when the boots are pushed into the toe strap. The rivets joining the heel straps to the toe strap are placed far enough apart so the ends of the toe strap can be twisted around the master cord of the snowshoes and then brought back up along the toe strap and in between the heel strap rivets, with the ends then tied together over the toe. The two trailing ends of the heel straps are tied or buckled together to form a large loop. Once the proper size of this loop is determined — based on boot size — no further adjustments need be made to either the toe or heel straps unless wetting or tension stretches the leather.

To use this binding one merely pushes the toe under the heel strap and swings the foot up so the end of the heel strap loop is resting at the instep. Then swing the foot out and around the outside heel strap and bring the toe up under the same heel strap and then into place through the toe strap. This process is a bit complicated to describe, but is simplicity itself in actual practice and the

F

This simple *native Alaskan binding* looks difficult to manage but one soon gets the knack.  *Suggested by Joe Delia*

real beauty of this hitch is the fact that one need not bend over to attach snowshoes to one's feet. With a bit of practice a person can get into this binding in a twinkling. Likewise, it can be jettisoned equally as fast and, if one should break through thin ice, this hitch can be a lifesaver. Walking on snowshoes using this binding certainly requires more skill than with the more rigid bindings, but Mr. Delia says, "we run behind dog teams, jump logs, wade brush, cut wood with our style of harness and don't notice any lack of control."

Another slightly more complicated harness which Mr. Delia mentioned uses the "Squaw Hitch." This binding (diagram G) utilizes a separate piece of leather for the toe piece which is woven through the lacing of the snowshoe on either side of the toe hole to form a loop through which the toe can be pushed. The main binding is a long thong of rawhide tied as shown in the diagram. According to Mr. Delia, "this is the most common method of attaching the foot to the snowshoe among natives (Indian and Eskimo) and white trappers in back country Alaska." This harness and the one described just above have the advantage of great simplicity. It is surprising that they are not used extensively in the northeastern United States. It would seem that these bindings could be used perfectly well in almost all situations — the main exception being for mountaineering which, as we have said before, requires a much more rigid binding. Perhaps this book will serve to disseminate information about them.

## For More Heel Control . . .

In fact, a similar binding is now on the market and has been available for a number of years, although we have not seen many of them in use. This harness (diagram H) is made of an aluminum and stainless steel footplate with leather straps. It was first developed for the commercial market by the Howe Folding Furniture Company of Norwalk, Connecticut. They were later licensed for manufacture in Canada and are now available through Bastien Brothers (see list of snowshoe manufacturers at the back of the book).

In appearance the footplates for these bindings resemble the letter U with the opening wider than normal so that the letter U is hybridized with the letter V. At the forward tips there are pivot

G

Simplicity itself — the *Squaw Hitch* — another native Alaskan binding makes use of just a long leather thong.

H

The metal heel piece is what gives this *heel control binding* its advantage.

points and attachment bars where the bindings are screwed directly to the frames in the case of narrow model snowshoes. In the case of wider snowshoes, the attachment is made directly to the snowshoe lacing. The leather toestrap is attached to the master cord separately from the rest of the binding. In fact, one of the major advantages of this design is the slight reliance on the toe strap. Only a very loose cinching of the toe strap is necessary which doesn't restrict circulation of blood in the foot as much as in some other harness models. At the rear of the harness another strap passes diagonally under the heel of the footplate and across the instep and hitches with a buckle on the outside. This strap is the main point of attachment and holds the boot back at the rear of the harness which is padded with leather for comfort.

This binding provides excellent heel control which is the main reason why it is so useful in mountaineering, eliminating entirely that tiresome slipping of the heel down-slope when one is making a traverse across a mountain snowfield. Another added advantage of this heel control factor is the ease with which one can turn corners, for with this binding the snowshoes stay in true line with the feet. A further benefit comes from the fact that, when the bindings are attached to the snowshoe lacing, the bolts that are used can be left projecting to act as crust spikes and eliminate, to some extent, slipping on icy surfaces.

The major disadvantage is weight for, even though made of light metals, these bindings are comparatively much heavier than other models of harness. Some of our correspondents have reported that the metal in these does not stand up under the stress of cold weather and heavy use, but in our experience these bindings have proven to be very satisfactory. Heel control is the major advance that these bindings contribute to snowshoeing technology and, if one intends to do any amount of snowshoe mountaineering, the extra cost is a good investment in comfort and satisfaction. Needless to say, the use of these bindings need not be restricted to mountaineering: they will be useful for all who make extensive use of snowshoes.

## Simple and Cheap

An old rubber inner tube from an auto or truck tire can be the source material for two other kinds of snowshoe bindings. The first, and simplest, is made by cutting off two crosswise sections from the tube to form a couple of rubber bands about half an inch wide each (diagram I). These rubber bands can then be combined with the toe straps of the snowshoes to make a quick and convenient hitch to keep the feet from slipping out of the toe straps. The handiest way to use this harness is first to slip the rubber bands over the boots up to the ankles. Then one steps into the toe straps so that the toes project through the straps. The rubber bands are then pulled forward over and then under the toes of the boots. The tension of the rubber keeps the feet from sliding back out of the toe straps. This type of harness does not give much heel control, but it does have the advantage of simplicity and cheapness and is perfectly adequate for short trips.

The other binding using rubber inner tubing is made by cutting out a flat section in the form of a trapezoid (diagram J). First a hole sufficiently large to push the feet through is made in the center. Then holes are punched through the corners at the wide end of the trapezoid, after reinforcing these corners with an extra layer of

A piece of old inner tubing makes a good heel strap for a *homemade binding.*

rubber. Rawhide is then laced through these holes onto the master cord of the snowshoe in such a way as to provide enough tension on the rubber so that the foot won't slide forward when it is in place between the rubber and the master cord. The small end of the trapezoid is then pulled up over the heel and that's all there is to it. Another simple and cheap harness.

At one time the Howe Folding Furniture Company of South Kent, Connecticut, produced and sold such a binding made of Neoprene, but we understand that this has been discontinued and know of no other supplier. However, this binding could be easily crafted at home, using a pair of heavy shears to cut the old rubber inner tube and an awl to punch the holes. Lest the reader be deceived by such seeming simplicity, we should add that these bindings tend to be too loose for much downhill traveling; that is, the foot will tend to slip forward since the binding does not hold the toe firmly in position over the master cord. Another drawback to this

J

Extra thickness of rubber where holes are punched

(bottom view)

13"

16"

1.

2.

3.

4.

5.

Old inner tubing also can be used to make this somewhat more complicated *trapezoidal* binding.

type of binding is its reaction to cold weather. Extreme cold will make the rubber stiff and difficult to manipulate. However, for those who like to experiment, this binding is worth the time it takes to make.

To close this section on bindings, let us offer an exotic touch based on the principle of the winter boots the Laplanders make of reindeer hide. As some of our readers may know, these boots are made in such a way that the toes turn up into a point with a slight reverse curve. The boots are made this way with the functional purpose in mind to provide a simple ski binding. By slipping the toe of the boot under the toe strap of the ski, the curved toe acts to hold the boot from slipping out backwards. It seems to us that this technique would work perfectly well as a snowshoe binding. The reindeer skin for these boots is tanned with the hair on and the boots are wonderfully warm and light, especially when they are used with a lining of dried sedge in the place of socks. Of course the main disadvantage for our readers is the difficulty of getting such boots in North America. Perhaps the time will come when outlets for these boots will be established here.

# Clothing
# and Sundry

## What to Wear

### Footgear

In planning clothing to wear snowshoeing, the best place to start is at the bottom with footgear. We believe the very best footgear to be the Indian type high moccasin worn over one light pair and one heavy pair of woolen socks. If your skin is allergic to wool, try wearing silk next to the skin. Silk socks are both warm and water absorbent, as well as being gentle to the skin, and are now quite readily available at most recreational equipment suppliers. If the moccasins are to be worn mostly in very cold weather it is best to get those that have been chrome tanned as these have a more open texture and are much the warmest. Oil tanned leather is more waterproof and better for temperatures near or above freezing, but oil tanning makes for colder footgear. These moccasins are very light and comfortable on the feet and, since they do not have heels, tend to be easy on the webbing of the snowshoes.

Next best, in our estimation, are felt boots and overshoes. Felt boots are even warmer than moccasins, but for long journeys they are not so comfortable as the felt has a tendency to raise blisters even when well fitted over good socks. Felt boots and overshoes, although not so commonly seen now as in former times, are still more easily purchased than the real Indian-type moccasins. In cold snow with temperatures at zero or below, the felt boots can be worn without overshoes in perfect comfort. The rubber overshoes are mainly

Five versions of snowshoe footgear: A, the chrome-tanned moccasin; B, the shoe pac; C, a felt boot which, when needed, can be slipped into D, an arctic; and E, a snowmobile boot.

useful to keep the felt from soaking up water when the temperature is near freezing.

Snowmobilers have been using a combination boot for their sport which can also be used for snowshoeing. The snowmobile boot consists of a felt inner shoe under an outer boot. The outer boot has a rubber bottom combined with a nylon upper closed at the top to keep snow from sifting down into the boot. The snowmobile boots were not really designed for walking long distances, but for short snowshoe trips they would serve satisfactorily.

The combination rubber-bottomed and leather-topped shoe pac has always been quite popular with snowshoers, but we feel that they are now obsolete. For an equivalent sort of boot, insulated rubbers are a better buy. Insulated rubbers are very warm, but tend to keep the feet moist because there is no way for perspiration to work its way through the rubber. Either insulated rubbers or shoe pacs are much heavier than the high moccasins or felt boots and the rubbers and pacs have the added disadvantage of heels which tend to wear down the snowshoe webbing rather quickly. Footgear with heels and snowshoes are a poor combination.

Some inveterate snowshoers wear only heavy woolen socks in even the coldest weather. The Norwegians make a sock-slipper which is intended for outdoor use. Although we have never tried this, we have no doubt that it would be ideal for snowshoeing in cold, dry snow.

## Next to the Skin

All clothing for winter wear should aim for lightness and dryness — all the way from footgear to headgear. This is a basic principle for winter clothing. Any form of physical exertion tends to create perspiration in larger than normal amounts and this perspiration must be conducted away from the body in order to keep skin surfaces as dry as possible. Of all the fabrics we know, wool is the best to wear next to the skin for this purpose. Yet most people cannot stand the itch. So, obviously, a compromise is in order. Various wool and other fiber combinations serve well and make comfortable underwear which should be of the convenient two-piece variety. Some find that the fishnet style underwear is good. The coarse, open weave of this fabric helps to allow perspiration to evaporate before it has a chance to soak into the other clothing.

## Outer Garments

For outer clothing, it is well to keep in mind another valuable principle — that of layering. Several light layers of clothing are better than one heavy garment. One or more of the light layers can be removed as your exertion increases in order to keep from getting overheated. Then, at rest stops, the clothing that was removed can be put back on to keep the body from chilling.

Trousers are best made of smooth, tightly-woven wool so that snow will not adhere to the material. Something cut along the lines

Young Girl Scouts and their leader in Anchorage, Alaska, bundled up for a cold-weather snowshoe outing. *McCutcheon Pictorial Service*

of cavalry breeches is good. These fit snug at the calf of the leg, but are loose above the knee. The junction between trousers and boots should be tight so that snow cannot sift into the tops of the boots.

For upper garments, a loose-fitting wool shirt is good to wear over your underclothing. Be sure that the shirt has a couple of good-sized pockets with button-down flaps to carry notebook and pencil, compass and whistle, among other things. Over the shirt could go a wool sweater or, even better, a down-insulated vest with a long tail to keep the kidney region really warm.

Finally, to cover the upper body as the outermost garment a good parka or anorak is indispensable. This should be of windproof, water-repellent material, cut rather full and with an attached hood. The pullover type parka is the warmest, but a little more inconvenient to put on and take off. The longer parkas reaching to just above the knee are good for warmth, but there should be a drawstring belt and some way to hitch the lower section up when you are walking, otherwise you will find it almost impossible to take a long step. A kangaroo-type pocket on the front of the parka is useful for stowing away odds and ends which should be conveniently at hand. All pockets should be zippered and, if a good long tab on the zipper is not provided, a short length of string or thong will be a most helpful addition.

## Headgear

Traditionally the snowshoer's headgear is, of course, the knitted tuque (pronounced tōōk). The tuque is of Canadian origin made with colorful woolen yarn and topped with a tassel. It is warm and light and in our estimation is by far the best for all kinds of winter sports. Its only disadvantage is the lack of a visor wide enough to shade the eyes from bright sunshine, so for sunny days we like to have a visored cap to wear. True, some knitted tuques do have visors, but these are generally not wide enough to be of much use.

## For Warm Hands

For covering the hands, in most cases mittens are better than gloves. For cold weather an inner and outer pair are best — the inner pair being of good woolen knit with the outer shell made of a tightly-woven cloth with leather palm and thumb. In our experience the outer mitten which has been made with a gauntlet and straps to draw the gauntlet up tight is very satisfactory. The gauntlet keeps snow from sifting down into the inner mitten (that is, if you remember to draw up the straps). For the absent-minded person, it may be best to buy outer mittens which have elastic bands sewn in to keep the gauntlet closure secure. When on a long trip, or when camping, be sure to include an extra pair of mittens. Some people also like to have a light pair of cotton gloves on hand. But get the gloves which have knitted wristlets.

Coureur de bois outfitted for a
cold day of hunting on
snowshoes. Note the com-
fortable *Squaw Hitch* bindings.

# New Materials

We realize that recent textile technology has advanced and
influenced the design and construction of winter sportswear to a
remarkable degree. Using basic materials such as down and
combining them with synthetic materials that breathe, new types of
clothing have been manufactured that make extended trips in severe
cold possible in relative comfort. Ski gloves have been designed that
now rival the warmest mitten combination. They are expensive but
widespread use will eventually bring the cost down. Warm-up pants,
made originally for ski racers, have been adopted by the recreational
skier and snowmobiler and prove very durable and worthwhile. The
full-length zippered legs allow for adjustments for wind and cold in
relation to the amount of movement required. The snowshoer too
can benefit from this feature and, because of their light weight,
warm-up pants can be carried without penalty and then fully utilized
when the snowshoer has to cross open stretches, against the wind.
They are easily put on and taken off. Being water repellent they have
proved a boon to the winter camper as he can work down in the snow
without wetting through. In addition they are very warm and most
appreciated when movement is limited or on rest halts.

One final point on the subject of clothing for snowshoers is to be sure that the fit is loose enough so as to not restrict body movement. An active sport like snowshoeing requires that clothing blend easily with the body so that your arms and legs can move freely and so that you can breathe deeply and easily.

## Costs

Perhaps it is not fair to go this far without giving the reader some indication of the costs involved in outfitting one's self for snowshoeing. And so, at this point we offer a few figures to give a rough estimate of current prices for the basic needs. However, we do so with considerable trepidation as this entire subject is very subjective. Many people would already have some of these items on hand and others of course can be purchased second-hand.

The prices we give here have been selected from a variety of camping and winter sport supply house catalogs. We didn't make any effort to look for the very cheapest. In many, hopefully most, cases it should be possible to shop for better bargains. So, take heart and, for what it's worth, here goes:

| | |
|---|---|
| Snowshoes — modified bearpaw | $30.00 |
| Harness for same | 10.50 |
| Moccasins | 15.00 |
| Socks, light | 1.95 |
| Socks, heavy | 2.95 |
| Underwear top - 2 ply thermal | 5.50 |
| Underwear bottom - 2 ply thermal | 5.50 |
| Shirt, wool | 17.50 |
| Trousers, wool | 21.00 |
| Suspenders | 2.95 |
| Vest, down-filled | 21.00 |
| Parka | 27.50 |
| Tuque, wool | 6.95 |
| Mittens, leather outer shell | 4.95 |
| Mittens, wool inners | 2.50 |
| Total | $175.75 |

## Supplementary Equipment

Snowshoes in themselves when equipped with good harnesses are complete so there isn't much to say about supplementary equipment, but there are some things worth mentioning which can make travel on snowshoes easier under certain conditions.

## Crampons

A slippery surface or hard packed snow on steep grades cause snowshoes to slip and slide unless some form of anti-skid device is used. Much the same as tire chains are used on automobiles, some type of similar attachment for snowshoes is definitely in order. For purposes of convenience in definition, we'll call these anti-skid devices for snowshoes crampons.

In most cases the snowshoe crampons are put on and taken off to suit the conditions but, as we mentioned in the chapter on bindings, in some cases the crampons are built in and always project below the lower surface of the snowshoes. Such is the case with the United States Army hinged-plate binding which has two claws made as an integral part of the binding, and with the Bastien heel-control binding, on which the bolts that hold the binding onto the lacing can be left projecting downwards to act as crust spikes or crampons. These designs are good for moderately slippery conditions, but in some cases will not be enough.

The Cascade-Sherpa snowshoe has a custom binding that is built into the Neoprene webbing on the same principle as the old Army binding. It features a crampon that comes in direct contact with the hard snow and ice and is the most effective binding we have seen for keeping snowshoes under control on steep and slippery mountainsides.

Some people use aluminum angle plates riveted to a piece of leather which in turn is lashed to the webbing of the snowshoes just behind the master cord in the center section. A single strip of this angle stock about four inches long by three quarters or one inch wide is good. This strip is put in position crosswise of the snowshoe and so placed acts to keep the snowshoe from sliding forwards and backwards. A further refinement would be to add a section of aluminum stock of the same size placed at right angles to the first to form a letter T. This somewhat more elaborate sort of crampon would then help to prevent sidewise slippage. A crampon of this sort could be carried along as supplementary equipment in the pack and put on and taken off as required.

A less sophisticated sort of crampon is a short length of quarter inch manila or hemp rope which can be wound spirally around the frame and tied off to the webbing. This is similar to the "Ruff-lock" technique which has been long practiced by Indian snowshoers. In their case, instead of using rope, they wound the frame with heavy rawhide.

If you should find yourself out on a slippery crust with none of these things, it is possible to break off a few tree branches to weave through the lacing of the snowshoes to increase your traction. This technique should be practiced with care so as not to damage the lacing: it's only for use as a last resort.

If you do have a pocket knife and a few lengths of rawhide thong, a somewhat better emergency crampon can be whittled out of a tree branch. Cut the branch long enough to span the width of the snowshoe at the widest part and lash the branch crosswise of the snowshoe at each edge. It will help if the twigs on the branch are left projecting slightly from what will be the underside of this temporary crampon; then, if the surface for the upper side is stripped flat and whittled smooth at the points where it will be lashed to the frame, this will help hold your emergency crampon in place.

Another form of expedient crampon can be improvised by putting several wood screws through the upper crossbar, leaving the points long enough to act as crust spikes. We are told by Joe Delia that this technique has sometimes been used in Alaska quite effectively.

## Poles

As we shall see in our section on how to walk on snowshoes, ski poles are handy things to carry while snowshoeing. If not a pair of ski poles, at least one makes a handy walking staff. Choose poles with shafts long enough to reach to the arm pits when the points are

An ice axe made more useful with the attachment of a ski pole basket.

resting on a hard surface like a floor. When they can be obtained the older poles with larger diameter baskets are to be preferred as the larger baskets give better flotation in soft snow. We often wind the pole shafts with tape at regular intervals so that the pole when inverted and thrust into the snow can act as a measuring instrument.

## Ice Axe

In snowshoe mountaineering an ice axe is perhaps to be preferred over ski poles, but in order to be most useful the ice axe should be fitted with a ski pole basket (see illustration). With a little remodeling the standard basket can be adapted to fit the larger shaft of an ice axe. However this remodeling is done, keep in mind the fact that the basket should be fitted to the ice axe so that it can be conveniently put on and taken off. Such baskets are easily obtainable from mountaineering supply houses. Obviously the ski pole basket would be a hindrance when the ice axe is to be used as it was intended. The ice axe can save you from a long slide down a steep and slippery slope so in high country the ice axe is a much better companion than ski poles.

## Handy Extras

We should also take note of a few other practical aids for snowshoers to carry along. These items are suggested elsewhere in the book as well, but they bear repeating. First and foremost is a good pocket knife equipped with a leather punch. Next, any snowshoer should always have at hand some lengths of rawhide thong or good nylon cord. Almost any field repairs can be carried out with a knife and thongs, but some also like to have a few short strips of one-eighth inch by one inch strap aluminum to use as splints in the repair of broken snowshoe frames. Soft wire or tape is good to use to hold the splint in place. A map and compass, and the ability to use both, are needed when traveling in unfamiliar country. A plastic police whistle is a good signaling device if you need to call for help. Don't forget to have matches in your pocket; the water-proofed wooden stick matches are by far the best for getting a fire started. And be sure to consult our chapter on winter safety for further tips for safe and happy travel in the winter woods and snowfields.

# Tips on Technique and Travel

Ask an old-timer how he learned to use snowshoes and he will likely reply, "B'gosh, I dunno, it seems as though it sort of came naturally." Here, in fact, is the great advantage snowshoes have, for the technique of traveling on them is practically as simple as walking on bare ground. No long training period is required and the novice becomes confident on snowshoes in a matter of minutes. The important thing to remember is that walking on snowshoes is like a normal walking gait on a hard surface with only slight variations.

## First Steps

If at all possible the beginner should learn with the aid of an experienced snowshoer on snow which the latter has prepared by tramping out a nice wide track. This serves two purposes for, while the instructor is tramping down the track, the beginner can observe how his teacher is handling the snowshoes. We recommend that the novice use the modified bearpaw of the Green Mountain or Westover design to begin with and that, at least at first, he or she use a pair of poles to help maintain balance and give a sense of security. Just before making the first step, the pole should be set out ahead and planted firmly in the snow. If, for example, the left foot is to be the first to move, the right hand pole should be planted out ahead, and a bit to the right, of the line of travel. The reason for doing this

73

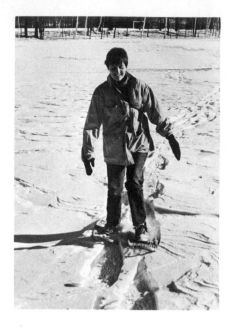

A beginning snowshoer taking her first steps across a snowy Vermont meadow. She already seems to have mastered the *cardinal rule*. *Robert George photo*

is to ensure two stable balancing points while one foot or the other is in motion. After a few sorties using this technique, the learner will find that it is no longer necessary to use the poles between each step and that only one pole is enough, except perhaps for steep ascents when the second pole will be most helpful.

## Cardinal Rule

The cardinal rule of snowshoeing technique is to remember to pick up the foot to be moved ahead *over* the edge of the stationary foot and to move this foot far enough *ahead* so it won't encumber the stationary foot. Obviously one cannot walk when one foot is holding the other down. Contrary to what might be expected, this mode of walking does not require one to keep the feet wide apart in awkward positions. A normal walking position is quite in order only remembering not to step on the edges of the snowshoes. With these few tips firmly in mind a novice quickly gains confidence on a well-packed track moving over level terrain.

After a student has gained this confidence and has achieved a sense of balance, he should move out ahead into the deep snow and get the feel of what it is like to break track. At this point it is important to remember to shorten the steps and keep the tips of the snowshoes from getting loaded with snow. By planting the snowshoe into the soft snow heel first one can avoid this pitfall and keep the tip unencumbered.

Likely somewhere along the way the beginner will take his first spill into the soft, deep snow and wonder how on earth he will ever get back on his feet again. Here the pole will come in handy for, if one can touch bottom so to speak, the pole can be used as a vertical prop. Then, once the snowshoes are in position the snowshoer can raise himself back on his feet. However, when the snow is so light, fluffy and deep that the pole cannot be used as a vertical prop, it can be used laid horizontally on the snow and, grasped at mid-point, still serve its purpose very well.

Of course we highly recommend that mutual aid be extended in these embarrassing moments and that the fortunate snowshoer still standing lend a hand to his beleaguered companion. Before attempting to get up, no matter how aided, the snowshoer should be sure to work the snowshoes into a position flat on the snow and, in the event that the fall took place on a slope, place the snowshoes in a position horizontally across the pitch of the slope. Trees and bushes are also invaluable aids to assist one in getting upright again after a fall. As a last resort, if the snowshoes seem hopelessly snarled and the snow bottomless, the bindings can be unhitched, the snowshoes taken off and set in a good position to use as a platform to get back on your feet again. Don't thrash around needlessly. We should all take a tip from oxen who lie quietly while their drivers arrange for them to get back on their feet, unlike horses who often get panic-stricken after a fall in the deep snow.

## Moving Out Uphill

Until now we have been describing the beginning stages of learning to snowshoe. Once a person has learned to walk easily over flat or gently rolling countryside either on a prepared track or in deep snow, and has become familiar with how to get back on his feet after a fall, he is ready to try ascents and descents. On a rather gentle

Two snowshoers moving out uphill make use of a rolling gait and step turn on their traverse.

slope one can climb straight up using the same technique as for flatland travel, but as the slope becomes steeper there are several pointers that can be applied. On a moderately sloping hillside the herringbone step can be used successfully. This step is made by toeing out so that the snowshoes form a slight angle to the pitch of the slope. It is not a very comfortable step to maintain for long and we recommend it only for short climbs on slopes of moderate degree. Another climbing technique is called "walking on your toes." In this technique the front of the foot is pushed through the toe hole of the snowshoes and dug in for a hard scrabble up the slope.

## Points on Traversing

For longer, steeper climbs the best technique is the traverse. On a traverse, the climbers make diagonal tracks across the face of the slope. Thus one decreases the steepness while increasing the distance traveled. On a steep slope of wide expanse each traverse can be rather long. For steep and narrow slopes the traverses will correspondingly have to be shorter zigzags. There are two important things to learn about traversing. First, while crossing a slope one must master the technique of edging the snowshoes so that they will rest horizontally when planted in position. Otherwise the snowshoer's ankles will soon tire and trouble with bindings will follow. The other point concerns the matter of making the turns at the end of each traverse.

## Edging

Edging snowshoes is not as easy as edging skis because of the added width of the snowshoes. Thus, in order to learn edging technique more easily, the novice should, if at all possible, wear the narrower style of snowshoe such as the modified bearpaw, trail or Alaska shoe. Then, crossing a slope, he should swing the heel over to the inside edge of each snowshoe and tramp down firmly at each step. On a slope of moderate degree one can create a snowshoe track allowing both left and right feet to be approximately level just by stamping the uphill snowshoe in with more pressure. However, as the slope becomes steeper, a separate upper and lower terrace may be necessary.

On such steep traverses one pole, or a pair of poles, can be invaluable aids to help maintain balance and to serve as a pivot point in making *step turns* around at the end of each traverse. Another useful aid when climbing on snowshoes is the ice axe — a standard piece of equipment with mountaineers. In snowshoeing across steep snowfields or on a slope with an icy crust (having taken avalanche hazards into consideration first of all) the ice axe is by far the best aid to carry for it can be used to arrest a long and perhaps dangerous slide to the bottom of the slope, whereas a pole is nowhere nearly as effective in such a situation. As we saw in the chapter on equipment, when using the ice axe in soft, deep snow — as is most likely on snowshoe excursions — it pays to modify it by adding a ski pole basket to the shaft of the ice axe at about four inches from the spike tip.

## Turning Techniques

The simplest turning technique can perhaps best be described by using the face of a clock for comparison. Suppose one is traveling on a traverse in the direction of ten o'clock and wants to change direction towards two o'clock. The change of direction is accomplished by placing the snowshoes in sequence, first right and then left, around in a clockwise motion. The tails of the snowshoes move least of all while the tips cover the most distance, similar to the hands of a clock. This simplest and easiest of all turns to master is called a *step turn* and as one becomes proficient at it he can make a rather sharp change of direction with only one step.

Should one need to make a sharper turn in order to go more directly back the way one came, the best way to accomplish this is with a *kick turn* — the same turn that skiers use and done the same way. Merely pick up one snowshoe or the other and turn it one hundred and eighty degrees. Settle this snowshoe firmly in place, then bring the other up and around beside it. It's as simple as that, but practice a few of these kick turns on a level, packed surface before attempting them on deep snow. Poles are very useful to help maintain balance when practicing kick turns.

## Body Movement

Most snowshoe travel takes place over a surface cover of either new soft powder snow or semi-compacted old snow — both of which allow each snowshoe to sink into the snow to some extent at each step. On such snow surfaces you will find that a very slight pause at the end of each step allows the snow to coagulate. This pause, when combined with an added downward moment of force, causes subtle changes to take place in the snow structure. The changes are such that each succeeding step will be made from a firmer base than would be the case if one tried to step lightly hoping to avoid sinking in so far. Another body movement that adds to the ease of snowshoeing is a somewhat exaggerated shifting of weight from side to side with each step. It is almost, but not quite, a lurching step and amounts to a rolling gait that is quite characteristic of woodsmen and is particularly useful in walking on snowshoes. But take heart, these movements seem to come almost naturally after traveling on snowshoes for a short time.

Three styles of downhill technique: A, leaning slightly backwards; B, using cord to keep from becoming mired in deep snow; and C, the easy, if damp, way.

## Downhill Travel

Travel downhill on snowshoes provides the ultimate test of bindings. The weight of the traveler tends to push his toe farther into the toe piece and often, if the toe strap isn't tight enough, the toe will slide under the cross piece and send him headlong into a face-first spill. It is best to judge the slope ahead carefully and select the technique best suited to the snow cover and the pitch. Generally, if the slope is not too steep, one can lean back a bit holding back the

full weight and putting pressure on the tails first. This technique will
get the snowshoer safely down moderate slopes. If the snow is firm
and the pitch steep enough for sliding, then place one shoe directly
ahead of the other and sit on the rear shoe and slide down. This is
easy when wearing shoes with a generously upturned toe.

The pole or staff can be used as a rudder or brake if the going
demands it. When using the poles as a brake, place them together
one basket over the other for added strength and control. Be careful
about where you put your weight, if too high above the snow it may
break the pole. Using the poles as a brake or rudder is ineffective if
placed on the shoe itself, no matter how hard one pushes, or if the
basket of the ski pole is overlapping on the shoe instead of in the
snow completely.

Should you come to a modest drop-off you may be tempted to
jump. Go ahead. You will fast learn that the tails will hit the snow
first and drop straight in while you will probably drop straight
forward or backward but in both cases horizontally. Should you
seriously want to jump while wearing snowshoes, tie the heel down to
the webbing; you can then land in a reasonably stable position. It is
worth a practice or two certainly.

## Poles as Aids

As we have seen, poles are helpful aids to snowshoes going both
uphill and down. There are two other functions they serve we should
mention. One is as an aid in backing up. As you can imagine, this
maneuver is next to impossible when wearing bearpaws and absolutely impossible with Algonquins or Alaskas without some aid to
push the toe of the snowshoe down so that the tail can be raised high
enough to get it up out of the snow backwards. A pole can be used to
hold the toe down just enough to do this.

Another use for poles is as an aid in carrying the snowshoes.
Place the snowshoes sole to sole and merely slip the handgrips of the
poles through the toe holes of the snowshoes. Pick up the poles as a
pair and hoist the snowshoes on the poles to your shoulder. The
baskets on the poles will keep the snowshoes from sliding off backwards. Of course an ice axe can be used in the same way.

Making use of ski poles to back out of a difficult spot.

Using poles as a pair is very helpful on steep climbs but as a rule only one pole is needed on most excursions. Even then, it is not always used as a walking staff but can be carried horizontally at the balance point or put over the shoulder. But take care when handling poles. They have sharp points and can cause painful puncture wounds and remember that the ice axe is triply dangerous in this regard.

## Cross-Country Travel

Once these basic techniques have been learned, the time has come to start out on some longer trips in small groups. Although we know a trapper or woodsman will often make extended solo journeys of long distances and seldom get into trouble, we strongly urge that snowshoe trips be made in small groups. This is a significant safety precaution, on top of which the pleasant companionship is an important consideration. While two people can manage nicely for short trips of an hour or so, we recommend four as the ideal number for longer excursions taking up the better part of a day or more. Then, if perchance there is an accident, one person can remain with the injured member while the other two go for help.

## Trail Breaking

When any group is out in untracked snow it goes without saying that the function of trailbreaker must be rotated from time to time, and frequently when the group is making a sharp ascent. There is no need for one person to assume the entire toilsome burden, even when the party is made up of a combination of expert snowshoers and beginners. After one person has had a stint at trail breaking he should step to the side and let the next in line take over. The former trailbreaker should wait until the rest of the party passes by and then take up a position at the rear of the group. The person directly behind the trailbreaker can also serve a useful function by not following precisely in the tracks of the leader, but by overlapping the leader's steps and thereby helping to create a smooth corridor in the snow for the rest to use.

As our readers will assume from what we have said above, traveling in Indian-file procession is standard procedure for snowshoers. However, when walking in Indian file, it is important to remember to keep a suitable interval so that one is not stepping on the tails of the snowshoes of the person in front. This seems to be a difficult lesson for some people to learn; perhaps the following trick for an exasperated snowshoer to play on the person who regularly treads on the tails of snowshoers will help. While passing under the snow-laden branches of a spruce or fir tree, give the branches a quick snap and jump from beneath to let the cold snow cascade down over the "tail-treader." All in good fun of course for we'd hate to be accused of sowing seeds of dissension in what would otherwise be a happy party. One bath of cold snow should be enough reminder that it is only courteous to keep a polite interval open. Traveling Indian file makes it difficult to carry on a conversation up and down the line — all the more reason to take frequent breaks to examine some interesting tracks in the snow or to speculate on the age of some giant old tree.

Traveling side by side on snowshoes, although wasteful of energy, does sometimes serve a useful purpose by creating a wide track which might later be used for cross-country skiing or for dragging a sled or for helping get a snowmobile out of a tight spot. If traveling side by side is for the specific purpose of making a wide track it is best done by not walking directly abreast, but by having the second man (third, fourth, etc., as the case may be) walk just slightly behind and to the side of the leader so that the tracks overlap at the same time as width is being added.

## Near Trees

In traveling under trees and near the trunks of them be extra careful of exposed bare branches in the snow especially if on a slope. Wood on wood is slippery and often the branch is icy. Also the bole of the tree may prove to have air-pocketed snow around it and let you down. People have been caught in a tree top thinking it was just a small tree or bush sticking up through the snow — a very dangerous position if alone.

## Gullies and Ravines

In our discussion of snowshoe travel thus far we have assumed a relatively smooth snow surface. But, while snow does tend to smooth out a lot of the rough spots and make for easier traveling, there will still be gullies to cross and other small irregularities of the terrain. In walking over this kind of country take care not to put weight on snowshoes that are only supported at the tips and tails. Snowshoes were not designed by bridge engineers and, while a well made pair will take an amazing amount of abuse, there is no need to put them to the ultimate test and run the hazard of a broken snowshoe. Bridging the snowshoes over gullies or getting the webbing snagged up in brush and dead limbs is to be avoided whenever and wherever by taking any extra steps required.

The gullies mentioned above are not the same as small ravines and brook valleys which of course must be crossed from time to time. In regions of deep snowfall, snowshoers may follow an established hiking trail provided with suitable footbridges only to find that the bridges are so piled with snow that getting across on snowshoes involves a balancing act on a narrow ridge. In such a case it may be worth the extra time to push some of the snow off or, if wearing the short bearpaw snowshoes, one can, if careful, walk across by putting one directly in front of the other. No one should tempt fate however and try to put on a sideshow tightrope act for the benefit of his companions. He might have to be hauled up wet and shivering from a fall into an icy torrent; or, even worse, end up with a broken limb.

## Over Ice

Brooks and streams bring to mind the subject of ice and how best to travel over frozen surfaces. Good, sound ice will support an enormous amount of weight and many winter roads are built to take advantage of good routes over frozen lakes and along ice-covered streams. Where these roads and trails have been laid out and marked by people who know their business they can be used with no fear until the spring thaws begin.

However, in most cases one will not have the benefit of such carefully marked winter ice roads so it will not be amiss to note a few of the hazards to be considered before setting out over snow-covered ice. A party of four traveling Indian file should have a minimum of two inches of good ice under the snow before venturing forth and should maintain an interval of fifteen to twenty feet between persons. Beware of gray spots on the otherwise white surface as these gray spots are sure indicators of places where the water is only thinly frozen because of warm water welling up to the surface from springs in the bottom of the lake. Also give wide berth to points where streams flow into a pond as these places are also often poorly frozen. Traveling over river ice is much more hazardous than over lake ice as moving water freezes very irregularly if it freezes at all and often a snow bridge will form up over moving water to camouflage a danger point.

It is only with a certain amount of trepidation that we suggest the possibility of travel over ice at all, knowing full well the hazards involved. But men always have and always will use ice roads so it would be foolish of us not to consider them and ways to travel safely over them. Just keep these extra hazards clearly in mind and be especially alert to the many dangers involved. Actually, the snow that does accumulate on large ice-covered bodies of water is quite apt to be hard and wind-packed thereby making the use of snowshoes unnecessary. The smaller, forest-rimmed ponds are the ones which usually collect enough snow to make snowshoes important means of transportation over them.

For those who may be making frequent trips out on the ice under varying conditions, the so-called Siwash binding (see the Joe Delia binding on page 54) is the safest to use because the snowshoes can be quickly kicked off if one does have the misfortune to break through the ice. When in doubt about the safety of ice travel, loosen your bindings before you cross. Loosen them enough so you can step out of them both instantly without having to bend down and use your hands. In fact, we recommend practicing this maneuver before crossing the ice. Another safety practice is to spread your group farther apart, as in avalanche territory. A coil of rope ready at hand and/or a long, slim pole carried by each traveler should be standard equipment for over-ice travel to help in rescue operations. And, of course, the rule of traveling in a group is especially applicable for journeys over ice.

## Another Extreme

The other extreme from ice, or snow that is hard-packed or with an unbreakable crust, is the very soft, light and fluffy snow blanket on which snowshoes don't seem to be of any help at all in keeping afloat. At least they seem of no help until one tries to wallow through such snow without them. If you must travel under such conditions try hitching a small section of light cord to the toe of each snowshoe — using the cord to pull the tip out of the mess whenever it becomes embedded. This same aid is also useful in the snow conditions often encountered near the end of winter when the snow has softened to such a degree that the snowshoes sink in too deeply to maneuver.

## Group Travel

As snowshoeing is again becoming more and more popular, more and more young people are joining in. Many Scout groups, 4-H groups and hiking clubs are recognizing that snowmobiles and trail bikes are fine in their place but that they do not replace the satisfaction of "doing it myself" on my own two feet — no mechanical aids needed. We would like to offer a few words of encouragement and advice to these young snowshoers and their leaders.

## The Sounds of Silence

To the young snowshoer on his or her first trip into the delightful and mysterious white stillness of the winter woods, it may come as a surprise to find signs of animal life there. But it is reassuring to see that their summer animal friends abound in winter as well. The proof is the countless number of tracks in the snow — as well as the deer yard signs. These tracks, many of which the youngsters may not recognize initially, seem to bond the young snowshoe traveler closer to nature.

So much has been written of nature and wild life in the spring, summer and fall that some may be inclined to feel that all nature sleeps through the long cold winters. It doesn't take many trips through snow-covered woods and fields to realize that this is far from true. While some animals hibernate others lead a very active life.

Deer tracks in the snow are fun to watch for.

The habits of the deer are especially interesting. These warm blooded animals often spend very tough winters as their tracks when they "yard-up" testify. Their yards are usually found where the brush and coniferous trees are thick and offer some protection and feed, and are characterized by narrow, hard-beaten paths criss-crossing each other in the snow. The bark and tips of the branches of the trees around these yards will be missing as high up as a deer can reach even by rearing up on its hind legs, and tufts of fur will be spotted clinging to the brush. Many off-shoot runs lead to other favorite feeding areas. These paths are so heavily trodden that one can walk on them without snowshoes. Deer will quickly utilize any path made in the snow, be it by snowmobile, skier or snowshoer, when it has hardened enough to keep them from sinking all the way to the ground. One only has to go back over his tracks a few days later to see.

Other things to watch for in the winter woods are the disappearing tracks of the field mice and shrews — tracks they make as they gleefully pop in and out of myriad tunnels they burrow to form an under-snow city as complex as man's. Then, too, there is the grouse. This bird often flies straight into a soft-snow drift to get itself completely covered with snow for a safe night's sleep, the lack of tracks helping to keep it undiscovered and the insulating properties of the snow cover serving as a warm blanket.

Not all signs of life in the snow-covered woods are quite so still and we should warn any spring snowshoers traveling in rocky, ledgy mountain country that any sign of bear dens should be a warning to retreat. A mother bear in spring, especially with cubs, is anything but friendly and can travel faster on her snowshoe wide feet than any snowshoer.

And so the youngster — as the adult before him — finds that the still woods are not still at all. The wind whistles through the pines, the tree trunks rub together producing eerie protesting sounds. There is the crack of a tree splitting in the cold, the whish of a tree bough springing free after losing its load of snow.

For the young traveler on snowshoes and in the woods for the first time just to fall down while attempting to back up on his shoes is an experience. How deep the snow is. How dependent he is on his snowshoes. To be able to travel on them at all is a wonder. Looking at his own tell-tale tracks leading from the distance right to himself fills him with the reassuring thought that, though in the wild, he is not lost and can always follow his own tracks back out. The young snowshoe traveler glows, reciting his adventures as though they had never happened to anyone else before. What a wonderful feeling this is. He long remembers his trip.

## The Leader

While individual youngsters will no doubt hack around on their snowshoes on their own, or with pals, any group snowshoeing endeavor for youngsters must have a leader. Winter travel in snow and cold off the highway requires more care and consideration than summertime travel and young people should have a qualified adult along, someone to assume the ultimate responsibility as well as enjoy the challenge and fun that all share. A true leader must have certain characteristics. Knowledge and experience, while necessary, can be acquired but integrity, an inherent consideration for others and a willingness to work harder than anyone else in the group are essential ingredients. A leader must have the judgment to know

Bobcat, on right, and red fox, at left, with their respective prints.

when to turn back, how hard to push to reach a safe place in the storm, an awareness of fatigue in the party — the real as against the feigned illness of a lazybones. Almost as important are the leader's ability to place his charges in a column of compatibility, his choice of a strong dependable "whippers-in" whom no one, repeat NO ONE, gets behind, and his resistance to the temptation to take unknown "short cuts" when time seems important but when safety should come first.

When no vital decisions have to be made a leader's willingness to consult with his group and share his knowledge develops group entity and the feeling of participation. Sharing his plans, route and reasons will be of definite value for future leaders when it's their turn and time to take over. Intelligent direction and division of trail breaking tasks by the leader will help produce instant confidence within the group. This sharing of the burden and fun of breaking trail is important.

These characteristics and principles of good leadership are old fashioned perhaps but tried and true principles which will never be computerized or supplanted. They will always be up to date in an ever changing world, albeit a shrinking one as far as wilderness areas go.

## Size and Safety

Groups for snowshoe travel needn't be large but should have at least four members, five if its members are still young enough to require a leader. As a rule, youngsters should be at least high school age to be on their own and even then only if they are resourceful, properly equipped and safety conscious. A group of 15 or 20 should have sub-leaders and the trip should be carefully planned to the last detail so that the law of averages — that something unpleasant will happen to someone — does not prevail.

The benefits of group trips with young people between the ages of ten and twenty are many. Much can be gained from day trips and even more from travel that may include an overnight stay, sheltered either in cabins, lean-tos, tents or snow pit shelters. Such experiences help young people find out who they are and how they stack up against their peers. They usually evaluate each other quite truthfully and at the same time gain an awareness of their dependence on each other and on their leader and of each's contribution to the group's well being.

Gaining confidence in one's own abilities is of immeasurable value to a youngster and the feeling engendered of kinship with others and with one's pioneering forebears, however distant, is enriching and soul satisfying. We believe that young people's groups where weather permits would do well to consider snowshoe tripping as a frequent activity and should work toward acquiring enough shoes so that their club or group could enjoy this activity to the utmost.

# Winter Safety

Travel on snowshoes in the winter snow and cold is wonderfully invigorating and a marvelous relaxation but it is not without its dangers. Snowshoers should be prepared to cope with emergencies — whether they be a broken snowshoe, an unexpected bivouac or a possible encounter with an avalanche.

The need for emergency repairs in the field must be considered routine. They should be planned for as simply, carefully and confidently as is food and water. Any leader — Scout, 4-H, mountaineer, snowmobile, or whatever — would be remiss and grossly negligent if not prepared to make repairs to snowshoers or their equipment and should be well briefed in this whole area before going into the field. There is no serviceman or wrecker out in the winter boondocks.

## Survival in the Snow

Any snowshoer going any distance into the winter woods or snowfields should plan to carry the proper emergency equipment with him. This should include a first aid belt, map and compass, flashlight, waterproof matches or fire starters, as well as survival rations and snowshoe repair kit.

True safety in the snow, as elsewhere, begins with prior planning. While it is not our intention to discourse here on how to camp, we do urge beginners especially not to start out without giving serious study to winter camping and hiking. We encourage them to check their libraries and book stores for good material on outdoor living in the winter. This material will stress leadership qualities, proficiency in map reading and compass use, common sense in reading weather signs and using forecasts and the standard practice of asking the natives about the terrain to be encountered.

91

Improvised emergency snowshoe using branches and twigs.

It will also stress that the people at home base be advised of the plans, which should include where the cars will be parked, expected time of return, contingency plans and alternate routes, etc.

Short hikes as shakedown cruises are heartily recommended; then longer trips. A winter practice campout in the backyard is not without merit. These efforts are all very worthwhile as the penalties for mistakes in the winter wilderness are apt to be severe.

## Snowshoe Repair

To be properly prepared to make emergency snowshoe repairs in the field the first step is to put together an adequate repair kit. The following is a good beginning: 1) wire, strong but pliable (copper or picture hanging is fine); 2) rawhide lacings and thongs; 3) a jacknife; 4) a fishline or 1/8" nylon cord, about 100 feet wouldn't be too long (if traveling in avalanche country, an avalanche cord might do); 5) a pair of lightweight pliers; 6) a roll of adhesive tape or electrical friction tape; and 7) a single-edge razor blade.

### Something Out of Nothing

The repair of broken snowshoes is not too difficult and has been discussed previously. But to replace destroyed or lost shoes, or to fashion emergency shoes where no shoes existed, is another matter. First, inventory the equipment at hand. Perhaps a pack frame, especially the packboard type, could be converted into a passable snowshoe. A simple snowshoe can be made from strong, straight green branches carefully notched and lashed. (See illustration.) The shape can be triangular or rectangular. It can be covered with regular cloth or ground cloth stretched as tightly as possible (sometimes something good has to be sacrificed). Smaller evergreen branches can be woven into the frame for support. A harness can be improvised by using these same branches lashed in a figure eight around the foot and the snowshoe.

As a last resort when no great distance is involved, fir or other coniferous branches can be lashed to the foot to serve as a shoe. The need for possible renewal of this type emergency shoe might make back-packing some extra branches a good idea if the trip still ahead will take you out of the right timber terrain. One other possibility is to try this arrangement: two people on three snowshoes. Simply tie one snowshoer's right foot and another's left to a single snowshoe.

Any extra time spent in deliberate and careful attention to making and strengthening emergency shoes will pay off in the end. Patience is a virtue too often ignored. Any leader — or individual snowshoer for that matter — should include in his routine planning ample allowance for unscheduled stops and bivouacs for repairs to either equipment or person.

## Survival Rations

A variety of emergency, or survival, rations are packaged in many forms. The work done on food for use in space has contributed much to this field as have the stories of survival in the arctic long ago. Several firms now put up very compact emergency kits. Chuck Wagon Foods of Newton, Massachusetts, to name one, puts out a kit consisting of compressed cereal bars, a starch jelly bar, non-melting chocolate bar, salt, single-edge razor blade, bandaids, wax-dipped matches, monofilament line, fish hooks, a piece of 12-by-18-inch heavy duty aluminum and a survival booklet, all in a waterproofed, nonsinkable package only 4-1/2 by 2-1/2 by 1-1/2 inches. Just reading the contents is inspiration enough not to get lost or in serious trouble. Space Food Sticks are another brand name item very good for use as an emergency food. Packaged in waterproofed paper, these sticks are similar to candy rolls but thinner and longer. They come in various flavors, are light in weight and abound in calories — a handful could help sustain one for many days.

Much lightweight survival-type food can be found in most supermarket food stores, which is where I discovered the space sticks. Lipton's, Borden's and Knorr's all make a variety of dehydrated foods that can be bought and kept to be used for emergencies only. They have long shelf life, take little space and are very lightweight. Beef Stroganoff, vegetable dinners, chicken dinners, cheese, ham and macaroni dishes, and the many varieties of soups are only to mention a few. Bouillon cubes should be a part of any survival kit as they are a good supply of salt which is often needed to help alleviate fatigue and muscle cramps.

## The Edible Wild

However, if the winter traveler should find himself lost in the deep snow and cold, he should take heart. Even in the deep woods there are edible foodstuffs at hand. The chief task is to convince himself that he can survive, or to "psych" himself up, to use the modern term. One of our friends, Don Jennings, who is an adviser to the Vermont State Police Mountain Rescue Team, suggests that the first step is to get hungry — that takes care of the fussy palate. Then look for anything that the birds are eating; one can usually eat what they eat (try a small amount first). Of course it might be better to catch and eat the bird. Other good emergency edibles are the nuts and seeds of the pine cones; the yellow tips of the new year's growth on the pine branches; the tips of spruce needles. One can use the tops of the cat-o'-nine-tails found in frozen swampy areas. Dig down and get the roots too. Boil this then pound it up to make a gruel. Wild apples can be cooked. Lichen scraped from rocks can be simmered, steamed and pounded into gruel. It abounds in food value if not in taste.

To be sure of these emergency provisions, go hungry the first day and then try a little at night. If you are OK the next morning, then go ahead and fill up. A warning though — sometimes this type of sustenance is constipating, sometimes it definitely isn't. Be that as it may, the snow traveler has a good chance to survive in the wild if he can stay dry and protect himself. He has the most necessary ingredient — water, or a form of it. It alone can sustain life without food longer by far than food without water.

## First Aid Measures

First aid measures are the same in the winter woods and snows as elsewhere, although the time factor involved in getting expert medical help must be considered and of course one should always be on the alert to protect one's own safety and that of one's friends when traveling off the beaten track in the winter.

Training in first aid is essential for anyone considering such travel and a knowledge of the effects of cold upon injuries and sickness should be a part of this training. Dr. Marlin B. Kreider's article, "Death from the Cold," is excellent source material. (First published June, 1960 in *Appalachia* magazine, reprints of this article can be obtained by writing to the Appalachian Mountain Club, 5 Joy Street, Boston, Massachusetts.) Assimilating this information is a must for all off-the-road travelers.

We should realize that the body works hard to maintain a constant 98.6 temperature and that when we abuse it, or overwork it or demand too much of it, we get into trouble. We lose body heat in four ways: (1) Evaporation, through perspiration which carries off body heat and precious fluids; (2) Convection, through exposure to the wind which swiftly carries body heat away; (3) Radiation, through the skin; and (4) Conduction, as heat flows to the coldest spot (we lose heat by sitting down or lying down on something colder than we are and, if our clothes are wet with sweat or the elements, they become an even better conductor of the heat to the cold).

Since the body can only produce heat in two ways — through food and exercise — we have to guard against an imbalance through excessive heat loss. If, when we are too tired to exercise or go on any farther, we sit down to rest, and at the same time take no food to balance the heat loss, we are in trouble. When we are in this condition our body temperature goes down and with it our circulation of warm blood to the extremities and to the brain. This results in a loss of thinking power and movement. If this continues in freezing weather or below we will die, it's that simple. So be conscious of heat loss and be sure to control it and avoid fatigue in cold situations. Be prepared with reserve rations and have dry clothes available or the means to dry wet ones. Snow travelers should watch each other for signs of frostbite when the wind is high and the temperature low. Freezing or frostbite shouldn't happen but, if it does, it's very evident. Frozen flesh when thawing out is very painful. Be alerted, however, that frostbite once thawed should not be used, bent or rubbed, but treated as a wound against infection and brought to medical attention. If it can't be treated immediately, it should be quickly thawed out and kept quiet until it can. "Frostbite," Bradford Washburn's excellent article which first appeared in the June, 1963 issue of the *American Alpine Journal*, is available through the Appalachian Mountain Club and should be on every winter traveler's bookshelf for re-reading each season.

## ABC's of Avalanches

The snow traveler, be he on snowshoes, skis, snowmobile or foot, must be aware of the potential danger of snow slides anytime he is in hilly terrain. Avalanches have influenced man's thinking in the snow country since before Hannibal and his ambitious adventures through the Alps. Nature causes most slides but man has contributed his share, wittingly and unwittingly.

Strangely, when the Italian and Austrian armies faced each other in the embattled Austrian Alps during World War I, more deaths were caused by manmade avalanches as part of the battle strategy than by shells and bullets. More than 16,000 casualties were reported from deliberate slides in one 4-day period. Man, through ignorance or calculated risk, still takes a grim toll of his own making on all continents where snow is piled up in sufficient quantities to slide when provoked.

There is no simple rule of thumb to gauge when and where a snow avalanche will let go; but there is a rule of thumb that says be ever conscious that the law of gravity is always in force. As Lowell Thomas says in one of the U.S. Forest Service's avalanche films "give it a mountain to slide on and enough snow and you'll have an avalanche."

Statistics are now being kept of all reported snow avalanches in the United States and it is becoming increasingly clear that the small slide on the small hill is as much of a killer, trapping the unbeliever,

Avalanche country. In spite of its peaceful outlook, this terrain — with its steep slopes and deep snows — is high-risk territory for the mountaineering snowshoer. *Gene Prater photo*

as the big mountain slide. In the so-called gentle mountains of Vermont in the winter of 1969-70 snow slides covered major roads, routes 12 and 14 to name two. That cars were not caught in them was sheer luck — luck induced by the fact that the slides came during a severe storm during which travel was restricted. Two youngsters were caught in a snow slide while playing on an open hill just outside of Barre, Vermont, a few years ago and, if it hadn't been for one of their companions flagging down a rural mail carrier — who ran to the site with a shovel and dug them out — it would have been fatal. They could not have survived another hour. In another not so happy instance just a few years ago, two New York boys were killed by a very small avalanche that came down on them through some brush on a 35 degree slope of only 300 yards.

If it seems that we are putting the cart before the horse in discussing these isolated incidents, before detailing snow slides in general, we are doing so deliberately. We want to dispell the average winter traveler's notion that "it couldn't happen here," or that such things only happen in the Alps.

It isn't just skiers or boys playing who get caught; unwary snowshoe travelers too have become victims. One such tale is told by Dale Gallagher in *Snowy Torrents,* a handbook published by the U. S. Department of Agriculture in January, 1967. One day about 1:00 P.M. three men from an electric company near Ashton, Idaho, went by snowshoes to repair an electric line at a radio relay station 12 miles from the nearest highway. They started across a slope about a quarter mile below the relay station when a 400-foot-wide avalanche released above them. One of the men saved himself by holding on to a tree, one man was completely engulfed by the snow, the third was injured by the crushing force of the snow but remained on the surface of the half-mile slide and was rescued, though later died of his injuries. It was 6:00 A.M. the following morning before a search party could reach the slide area but by noon 70 people were engaged in the rescue effort. At 12:30 a snowshoe was found and a half-hour later the body of the missing man was located under five feet of snow. He was nearly three hundred feet from where the slide first caught him and forty feet in from the edge of the slide. The snow was piled over twenty feet deep at this point. There was a deep gash on his forehead and some snow had melted about his mouth indicating that the victim may have lived for a short time. If so, his fate was another sad result of the fact that rescue operations timely enough to recover buried victims are almost impossible in inaccessible areas.

This is only one more of many such avalanche disasters and is mentioned for the sole purpose of reminding the reader to take the possibility of avalanches seriously on all field trips.

## Avalanche Causes

What conditions act to cause avalanches? In order of importance they are: snow conditions, shape of the slope, steepness of the slope, weather, growth or vegetation, and exposure (direction the slope faces).

### Snow Conditions

*New Snow.* Enough loose new snow on a hard base may slide on slopes of 25 degrees. An accumulation of 12 inches is considered sufficient providing the old base is slippery enough (ie., a hard sun or rain crust).

If the snow were dug down to ground level a profile of the many layers of snow from past storms would be visible. It would show what happens to the snow in its transition from new snow to ice. At ground level may be found what is called depth hoar, small ice cups like hollow hail stones. This depth hoar is caused by moisture in the snow interacting with temperature changes from ground heat — alternately melting and freezing. Depth hoar sometimes builds up to many inches and provides a very unstable surface on which new snow can cling, however precariously. Whenever falling snow builds up on this surface at the rate of an inch an hour or more it is considered dangerous and may slide anytime it is disturbed.

*Wet Snow.* Wet snow slides can be especially devastating even though they slide more slowly and at a more predictable time. This is because they quickly solidify to a concrete texture when they stop.

Wet snow slides are common in the springtime and occur in the same paths year after year. However, if the snow has built up and rain and warm winds combine, a wet snow slide can be expected on steep slopes at any time of the year, just as mud slides may be expected after extensive rains in certain areas on the California coast.

*Snow Slabs.* Avalanches which are formed from snow which breaks off in large blocks and in clean fracture lines are called wind slab avalanches. They are so named not because wind triggers the slides but from the fact that the slabs are formed by wind action. These slabs are usually found on lee slopes and are formed either by blowing snow being dropped on a lee slope or by a warm wind blowing across the snow into a slope, in either case causing the snow to compact in such a way that it locks to itself but not to the snow layer beneath. Usually an air space forms between the slab layer and the under layers. This slab condition is easy to detect (if there is no new snow on top) because it has a dull chalky appearance and does not reflect light. It may be a few inches thick or it may be many inches thick and may well support a man walking. The danger is not knowing what may trigger a fracture of this snow cover. It slides in blocks, quickly gathers momentum and most often carries any loose snow under it along too, at times down to ground level.

*Snow Cornices.* Cornices are made in a similar fashion to slab but are formed at the top of ridges by wind blowing the snow towards the edge of the ridge. This snow clings to itself and builds a false ridge which may extend a few feet out in space. It takes beautiful shapes and makes a lovely picture but it is treacherous and unstable, especially if you walk on it or are caught under it when it breaks off. And, if the conditions are ripe, when it falls it often starts the snow below to slide as well.

### Slope Steepness

Extreme steepness of slope is not always a principal factor in snow slides because anything steeper than 60 degrees avalanches almost continually thereby keeping the snow from building up to dangerous depths. Furthermore, anything that steep should make

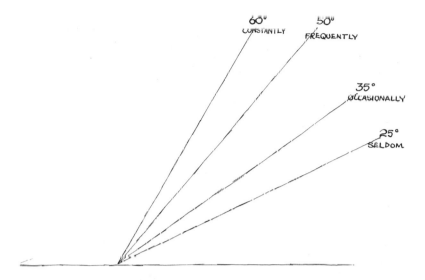

This diagram forecasts avalanche probabilities according to the degree of slope involved.

even the most unwary look twice and not get caught. However, slopes anywhere from 25 to 75 degrees *are* susceptible to snow slides.

### Slope Shape

An important thing to keep in mind is the shape of the slope. When a slope's profile shows its shape to be convex, the most tension on the snow cover would be at the top of the curve (although slides on these slopes have been known to break at the lower transition point). A concave slope would have the most pressure at the foot. On a uniform slope, the fracture line, or starting point, could be anywhere there is mass enough above waiting for the right trigger. And of course any slope may have any combination of these shapes.

### Vegetation

The vegetation under the snow cover may be as influential in bonding the snow cover as any growth still appearing above the snow line. Long grassy slopes offer no inhibition to slides. Scrub growth,

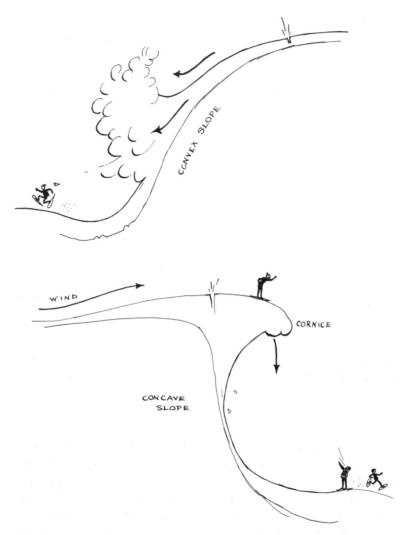

Slope shape plays an important role in the making of avalanches. This diagram shows a convex and a concave slope: both can be dangerous.

short grass, well-anchored rock and very uneven ground offer good anchors until the snow depth covers it all and you have a new surface. Heavy timber usually is a deterrent to free-flowing snow slides, unless the snow gets a good start from high open slopes way above.

Hummocks, gullies and ravines help break up an area and cause the snow to compact and anchor itself as it folds into the ground.

## Weather

Weather conditions are a strong factor in avalanche making. Once avalanche conditions exist all that is needed is a trigger and often that trigger is a weather change. A rapid rise in temperature after a heavy fall of wet snow on an old base could cause the melt to lubricate the old surface, making conditions ripe for a wet slide. A rapid fall in the temperature after a fall of new powder snow would prevent the snow from settling and bonding, making a slide most likely, providing all the other ingredients — mass, shape, steepness and lack of barriers — are also present. Another factor to be considered under weather is the wind which can aid in settling the snow or in helping to produce slab conditions.

# Triggers

What is needed to release a slide? All that is needed is something to break the sometimes delicate bond or cohesion of the snow — perhaps the shock waves from some sound, an abrupt change in temperature, an overload of snow causing the force of gravity to win over cohesion, the shearing of the snow cover by a skier or snowshoer or some snow vehicle. Any of these things, under the right conditions, can trigger a slide.

## Slab Snow Slide

It may only take a skier's or snowshoer's weight cutting the snow to cause a slab snow slide. The fracture line appears instantly and audibly (with a dull whumpf) as the air is compressed under the weight of the slab as it settles and breaks.

## Dry Snow Slide

A sound wave alone can trigger a dry snow slide. Even a loud shout has been known to start one. This type of slide starts at a point and rapidly fans out as it speeds down the slope often in excess of

100 miles an hour and with an accompanying snow dust cloud. The high speed causes air turbulence strong enough to pick up bulldozers, dump trucks and even houses, moving them or smashing them to pieces. Speeds have been clocked at over 200 miles per hour.

### Wet Snow Slide

These slides are not necessarily triggered but occur when enough weight succumbs to the pull of gravity.

A snow cornice breaking off from above can trigger a slide. Or ice hanging over a slope and falling on the snow beneath, with the added weight just enough to upset the balance. The sonic boom of an aircraft has been known to start a slide.

Happily, man's own devices can cause slides where and when wanted in order to make certain areas safe. Explosives in the form of artillery shells, compressed gas guns, or hand placed charges can be used to clear unsettled snow from threatening slopes. This is done by the daring but soundly trained Snow Rangers of the U.S. Forest Service.

## Travel Precautions

There are certain precautions which should be taken when traveling in avalanche prone terrain. One should always survey the territory as one goes. Estimate slope steepness and check slope exposures. Determine prevailing wind directions and choose the windward slopes: they are safer. Look for signs of small slides, "sloughs," which indicate avalanche conditions are present. Do not travel in a narrow-bottomed valley with avalanche prone slopes above you. If crossing a suspected slide area, cross as high up on the slope as possible. Cross one at a time, staying behind natural barriers (that is, below them) so as not to be swept against one. The slides may flow around such obstacles. If in a group, someone should be appointed to watch the slope above while the rest are picking their way across.

When crossing the slope itself everyone should loosen their gear and snowshoe bindings to enable them to throw everything off in a split second if necessary. A scarf should be worn around the face to cover the mouth and nose to prevent snow dust from getting in the airway in the event of a slide. Further, all should have a colored avalanche cord trailing out behind them; the theory being that the cord would bounce along on the surface of any slide and, being light, would stay on top. The searchers would then hopefully spot the free end and find the victim at the other end. This cord is usually nylon, about thirty to fifty feet in length and 1/8 inch in diameter.

## Helpful Hints

If you should be engulfed in sliding snow there are some helpful movements worth trying. Use a swimming motion with the arms and hands kept up near the face and try to stay on your back. An abbreviated breast stroke is recommended, much as you would use for swimming from under water to the surface, except for the leg kicks. Keeping the hands near the face helps to create an air space and to avoid having the hands pinned down. (Many suffocation deaths in the snow are due to lack of air space and from the snow being crammed down the mouth and air passages.) Staying on your back facilitates your trying to dig yourself out.

Dig slowly if it is at all possible to move the snow. You can determine which way is up by the pull of gravity on something held up to dangle, such as a watch strap. Don't be surprised if this shows you to be upside down. Sound does travel in snow but do not shout or scream until you hear someone looking for you. Breathe as quietly as possible to save energy and air.

At the same time your companions should be probing for you with whatever instruments they can find (ie., ski poles, staffs, etc.). The search should start from the last spot at which you were observed and work down the fall line scuffing the snow and probing, looking for clothing or equipment and stopping to holler every few steps. This should be continued for an hour with careful watch for more slides being kept all the while. Outside help should not be sought for at least an hour if it would seriously cripple a speedy search of the area. After an hour, if party strength permits, two should be sent for help; no one should travel alone unless absolutely necessary. The remaining party members should recheck the pile-up area and any areas where the snow may have been diverted around an obstacle.

When you (or anyone) are found buried, the rescuers should dig carefully with their hands when near the body. Standard first aid procedure upon recovery is self-evident, with special attention to the need for artificial respiration and the rewarming of the whole body. Exposure to cold and the subsequent lowered body temperature is inevitable.

## The Odds

The grim statistics show that chances for survival for anyone buried under more than two feet of snow for more than an hour are only about thirty per cent; for anyone buried in less than two feet there is about a fifty percent chance of successful rescue, if it is accomplished within half an hour. For those who like long odds, survival has been recorded up to seventy-two hours. In one extremely rare case in Norway, a successful rescue was recorded after the victim was buried for one week in a springtime wet snow slide. All these long-term burial survivals were by victims who were conscious and who did not have ice masks form to cut off their air (ice masks form around the mouth from exhaled breath from the mouth or nose which condenses and freezes when the victim is unconscious). And, in the Norwegian case, brush had provided air spaces and an airway through the snow above.

It is not the intent of this section to offer an avalanche course or furnish all the answers. However, it is its intent to create enough interest to lead the reader to seek out and attend a course or orientation lecture on avalanches, such as usually offered by local National Ski Patrol avalanche instructors or by Forest Service personnel. Write them or check with your local club but do keep yourself posted, and do obey all avalanche warning signs posted in mountain terrain.

## Winter Rescue

Each year there are many emergencies requiring search and recovery operations in all types of snowy terrain — mountainous, rolling, wooded and open. Much attention has already been directed to the forming of trained and equipped rescue units to work over the entire snow-belted North American continent. This has paid off but the demand still exceeds the supply. As more and more people hit the snow country on skis, snowshoes and snow machines, more and more emergencies are inevitable — to say nothing of the incidents involving downed airplanes, lost hunters, snowbound travelers and stranded mountain climbers.

Emergency recoveries in snow country have been aided greatly by dependable over-snow machines. Sometimes, however, the machines fail or get bogged down or the operator gets hurt and any would-be rescuers are back on their own two feet again. As snow over a foot deep is too tiring to walk through, snowshoes are still the best answer.

Rescues come under several different headings:

A. Unplanned — usually on a small scale, perhaps from a sudden call from friends.

B. Self Rescue — an individual or his party is stranded.

C. Pre-planned — an organized effort by a trained rescue unit (National Ski Patrol, Air Search and Rescue team, Civil Air Patrol, etc.).

## Unplanned Rescues

These are regretfully more common than realized. Such a rescue might happen like this. A friend's wife calls about suppertime to say that her husband hasn't returned from his snowshoe trip though he'd said he'd be back several hours before dark. And off you go. What you need is a friend or two, equipment for the weather, headlamp or flashlight, first aid kit, emergency repair kit or, better yet, a spare pair of snowshoes and a map of your friend's favorite tripping area or someone who knows the area well. A voice gun might be helpful if you can get it in a hurry. Chances are that Jack has broken a snowshoe and is floundering along so hopefully it will just be a matter of trying to pick up his tracks. Take along some hot tea or bouillon. Flavor the tea with a generous spoonful of honey for quick energy. Your friend may be tired and this form of pick up is far better than the variety loved by many but better saved for when the rescued and rescuers are safely back indoors.

## Self-Rescue

The chief essential in this situation is prior training and use of the skills involved in survival living. This means always carrying all necessary items for emergency repairs to equipment or self, along with a reserve food pack and extra garment for the nighttime chill. Fire making tools would prove handy for making signal fires should you be disabled or just for morale boosting. Your map and compass would be an integral part of any self-rescue. Though it's worth saying that sometimes in these situations one is not lost — just confused. In this case, the best thing to do is just stay put for the night.

Once a decision has been made to go no further there are certain basic steps to be taken. (1) Try to assess the situation calmly. (2) To the best of your collective knowledge, decide where you are. (3) Figure the time it took you to get where you are from the last known source of help and/or shelter, realizing that it would take that much time or longer to get back, depending on the terrain, visibility, worsening snow conditions or breakdown of equipment necessary for movement. (4) Estimate your remaining daylight hours. (5) Make an inventory and pool all available resources, to include food and water, equipment in your pockets, any extra clothing, etc.

Then, under the assumption that this is strictly an emergency bivouac in *wooded* terrain and that you have neither sleeping bags, ground cloths or tents, first pick a spot to make camp by seeking natural windbreaks, such as under trees, against large boulders, or in burrows under blowdowns. Once the spot is picked, pack down the snow and gather wood for a fire. Remember that you are now concerned with survival, not ecology, so gather whatever insulation material you can find: boughs, branches, grass or bullrushes found by digging under the snow — whatever is dry. Then make a place to

sit down rather than to lie down. The seat should be as low as
needed to get out of the wind. Pad the seat with whatever is
available so you will not melt the snow under it or get wet in any
way. Put some insulation material down underfoot to help keep
everyone's feet out of the snow. Build your fire only after each
member has a place and you have gathered enough wood and that
much more again.

It is essential to conserve energy so all this preparation should
be at a slow pace. This will help keep everyone calm and prevent
working up a sweat. Stay together, assign tasks and rotate them. If
you have not eaten, once your protective shelter and fire place are
prepared and the wood gathered, fix a meal, but remember to keep
a reserve of food according to your estimate of how long it may be
before you get back to shelter. You need the food for energy and
heat. Ration it fairly and according to needs. If there are exhausted
members, they should be fed first, kept warm, and made to conserve their strength. Do not work until exhausted and, at all costs,
keep dry (wet clothes conduct body heat away faster than dry ones).

Once you have eaten, sit close together to share body heat.
Rotate the chores and the fire watch, letting the others doze off. In
addition to feeding the fire, the fire watch should keep tabs to be
sure that any clothes drying or feet being warmed are not too close
to the fire. The fire watcher should also have a good fan to stir up a
draft whenever the fire gets low.

Morning will come after what seems a very long night, but with
it will come fresh hope and new ideas of what to do (i.e., stay put
and wait for help or try to work your way back). If the decision is to
leave, consider how you might safely lighten your pack. Decide
what is absolutely necessary for travel and safety, leaving the rest in
a well-marked spot. A lighter load can make a big difference on the
return trip.

If the decision is to stay, or the group is in trouble, signal fires
can and should be prepared. The decision as to when to light them
should be based on the availability of more fuel, the time that
people may be searching, the presence of aircraft, etc. Green wood
and boughs will make smoke dense enough to be seen if the wind
isn't blowing too hard. The fire should be laid in as open a spot as
possible. The use of a signal mirror should be practised so that it

can be quickly focused when the occasion arises.

If caught in the open without cover or shelter of any kind, whether above timberline or not, the necessary self-rescue procedures will, of course, have to vary. Shelter from the wind is the first priority. Dig down to construct a snow slit trench, or if you can not dig down, build up. A snow wall built in the right wind direction will prove itself.

All the steps for emergency bivouac in timber apply here with the obvious exceptions of doing without a wood fire and without the insulation from gathered wood materials. Care must be exercised to protect against getting clothing wet when digging in the snow and handling snow blocks for wall building. Rotation of jobs should include checking each other for cold symptoms, injuries and degree of consciousness. The sit instead of lie down idea may have to be discarded and huddling together for warmth practiced in earnest. Every bit of insulation material must be utilized. If there is enough snow to construct a shelf to sleep on, it is worth the effort. Roofing the shelter may be possible with what is at hand. The snowshoes themselves can be used to provide a barrier between the snow and the user when lying down, or to provide roof support upon which snow can be piled to help trap escaping body heat in the shelter. Any external source of heat, even the heat of a candle, can be significant.

## Pre-planned Rescues

In a situation involving a pre-planned group rescue some official body of authority would assume the overall responsibility — whether it be the Police, Fish and Game Department, U.S. Forest Service, or whatever. Members of these groups are well trained in this work and would of course do the planning and directing. However, they often call on volunteers to help and it is our hope that the following might prove helpful to any seasoned snowshoer who might want to join such a rescue operation.

Once an emergency has been declared certain information is essential before a reasonable plan of action can be formed. What happened? Where? When? Who is involved? What is the probable cause? Every effort must be made to get the answers to as many of these questions as possible before the rescue plan is drawn up.

The director of the operation must choose his field leaders and brief them as thoroughly as possible. Speed is important but not always the paramount consideration. This briefing would include the following: 1) a statement of the operation's objective in as much detail as possible; 2) an estimation of the situation, including time, weather, terrain, support groups, chances of success, degree of urgency, etc., 3) an outline of the plan, giving group assignments, areas of responsibility, etc. As the same time the administrative details concerning such things as equipment, food and personnel would be covered, communications arrangements outlined and safety precautions gone over.

### Headquarters

A headquarters must be established — generally at the end of a road, the last spot wheeled vehicles can reach. This can be a house, school, camp, tent, bus, etc., but hopefully something heated with enough room for the workers, press and next of kin. It should also include a supply depot for all the necessary equipment and, if at all possible, medical help should be available. Sometimes, in an area that might attract sightseekers, even restraining lines must be provided.

A communications center should be established where messages can be logged in and out and a chronological account kept. A Situation Map should be adjacent to the log to mark the field parties' progress, pinpoint new areas and block out those already screened.

A word might be said here about the necessity for consideration of the next of kin concerned in these rescue operations which can sometimes become tragedies. Cruel or careless talk or expressions of doubts as to the efficiency of the operation must not be allowed to reach them. It only adds to the worry and heartbreak.

### Getting Ready

Before rescuers can be dispatched, they must be equipped. Each rescuer should have his own emergency kit, to include — as we have said before — snowshoe repair items, spare thongs, jackknife, light, extra clothing, food and a compass. He should also have a map premarked with known landmarks and zones of responsibility and signaling devices as planned. Group equipment should include the rescue sleds or ahkios with hauling harness, axes, saws, machetes, first aid equipment, notebooks and pencils, and perhaps lightweight stokes litters with material to convert them to sleds. Lightweight but strong shovels are a must, as are ropes for steep terrain and ice areas and perhaps for crossing doubtful frozen ponds. Snow vehicles, when available, should also be included, along with portable stoves for cooking and heat if necessary, with gas for same.

### Trail Breaking

The method of operation would depend upon the leader's instructions but prior practice in hauling sleds, breaking trail and controlling sleds on difficult terrain would be invaluable and eliminate any surprise as to how hard the going can be in these situations.

Trail breaking and sled or. toboggan handling in rescue work can be eased with thoughtful planning and careful attention to terrain and route selection. Consider the following: the rate of travel for a snowshoe column in unbroken snow cross country in variable terrain is about 1 to 1-1/2 miles per hour; on a broken-out trail, 2 to 2-1/2 miles per hour. Minimum safe thickness for safe ice crossing (in single file) on foot is 4 inches, perhaps 1-1/2 to 2 inches when on skis or snowshoes. Wet snow or water under the snow will cause difficulties as it tends to freeze to the webbing, adding considerable weight and loss of stability; in these cases the trail should be broken out and reinforced with brush and boughs.

When the trail is to be used by sleds (man hauled), it must be broken out even if speed is essential. The sleds will ride higher, haul easier and flotation is better. To break trail for sleds at least three people should do the job. The leader (or point) trying to hit the center line of the planned route and the two follow-up trailbreakers covering one of the leader's tracks with his inside foot and making a new track with his outside foot. This will result in a track at least four shoes wide. This is usually wide enough for a sled team hauling in single file. If possible pick the snowshoe to fit the terrain and snow

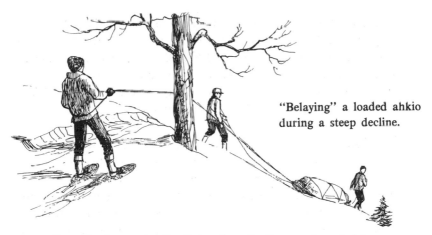

"Belaying" a loaded ahkio during a steep decline.

cover. Swap leads constantly. Set a time limit, no exhausted heroes needed.

## Sled Handling

Pick routes that for the most part lead straight up and down the steep sections. This will avoid sideslipping and off-the-track relay lines. On very steep sections ropes can be utilized to belay around trees in the line and allow for rests while holding the sled in place. The sleds should be hauled by men in file, using harnesses made (or improvised) to allow the pull to be straight back from each hauler without cutting off his wind or pulling on his stomach. The hands must be left free to dig in with the poles to add traction when necessary. The belay technique can be utilized to control the descent of the sled on steep pitches. Sometimes two "tail gunners" can be used to advantage when going downhill, with only one in front to keep the sled in line. On a traverse it may be necessary for men to be placed uphill and to the sides to control sideslipping with additional ropes. No one should try to haul a sled for any but short distances with just a rope held in the hands. Tying a loop in the rope big enough to allow a bight to go over the shoulder would be an improvement on the hand-held technique. The loop over the shoulder would allow the hands and arms to be free to use the ski poles as mentioned. This technique can also be used effectively with more than one man. Three can haul a 200 lb. load without too much trouble under favorable terrain and trail conditions. Hauling a sled with a casualty on it naturally requires considerably more care and attention. When establishing a route to the casualty, thought should be given to utilizing the same trail on the way out. Surveyors' yellow plastic marking tape can be used to indicate rescue routes. Yellow is best as it is unmistakable to colorblind people and is fast becoming accepted as the best for emergency use. When the rescue route is no longer needed, the tape should be removed to avoid confusion.

Some traverses may require that the trail be made level in order not to aggravate an injury by tipping the sled too sharply. On a steep icy trail a fixed rope may prove useful and the time spent establishing it well worth the while. This is, of course, if trained mountaineers are available. It involves a rope handrail anchored to trees or rocks, keeping the rope taut and about waist high to act as a handrail. It can be used to tie in to so rest halts can be made on these steep slopes without fear of losing the sled. The sled itself can be tied in to the rope. Prusik slings will ensure that the sled will not get away if the load has to be belayed up or down, snaplinks or carabiners are also useful. Installations of this type are a great help for operations in the dark or on slippery terrain and for weary climbers carrying heavy loads.

When hauling a casualty rescuers should keep their voices down when discussing terrain and other difficulties. Be sure the casualty's hands are inside. Someone near the head should be assigned to keep an eye on the victim, to converse if necessary and to cheer up as required. The victim's face should be watched for any change in condition and any displaced snow kept off his face and body to eliminate as much chilling and wetting as possible.

In the cold, frequent short 30-second to 2-minute rest breaks for breathing "blows" are better than infrequent but longer ones. Change crews on schedule and be sure to equalize the work load.

### The Wrap Up

The rescue effort must come to an end at some point, hopefully with success. But successful or not, there is always the tiresome job of cleaning up all the details. A report must be written, agencies notified, equipment returned, expenses taken care of and workers checked-off and thanked — all a necessary part of this important and demanding work.

# Fun for All

## Snowshoe Racing

Fortunately not all group activity on snowshoes is as grim as rescue work can sometimes be. A lot of fun can be had as well. Races on snowshoes have been held ever since man has had uncommitted time to use for recreation, and perhaps even before that. Although there may be many earlier examples, we know for a fact that snowshoe races were a big attraction as early as 1911 at the first Intercollegiate Winter Carnival held in the United States at Dartmouth College.

The guiding light in the matter of promoting snowshoe races has been the Canadian Snowshoe Union which, in affiliation with the United States Snowshoe Union, formed the International Committee which established the racing and marching rules and regulations. Some of the interesting features of these races and marches are described here to encourage others to try their skills and enjoy this angle of a great sport.

A "March" is a competitive distance event in which more than one racing club enters a team. A team usually consists of at least four members and they must *all finish* in order for the team to score. As in a cross-country foot race, points are awarded according to the place finished, one point for first place, two for second and so on — the winners being those with the lowest score. The teams are required to march in their club uniform. Although racing pants may be worn, the teams are required to march in their club jackets and tuques.

Speed events for men include races of varying distances such as the 100-yard and 220-yard dash, along with the longer 440-yard,

Only a few more steps to go. No. 83 approaches the finish line at the World Championship Centennial Snowshoe Meet held in Ottawa. *Canadian Travel Bureau*

880-yard and full mile races. The 120-yard low hurdles are also run (called obstacle races). Distance events include the mile, three-mile, 10-mile and 18-1/4-mile endurance races. There is also a Forced March which is usually 5 miles long and has to be covered by the entire team.

Events for women include the 60-, 100-, and 200-yard dashes, a 100-yard low hurdles race and a 1-mile forced march.

These snowshoe racers show excellent form and really cover ground at the Pas-Trappers Festival. *Manitoba Archives*

## Rules & Regulations

With a few exceptions, the conduct of the races conforms to that of most other foot races. Footgear must be the Indian-style moccasin. All snowshoes must be made of wood with gut or rawhide lacing. The foot must be attached to the snowshoe at the toe only, leaving the heel free.

Men's racing shoes must be at least 10 inches wide, measured from the inside of the frame, 33 inches long and must weigh no less than a pound and a half. The marching snowshoes for men must be no less than 40 inches long. Ladies' snowshoes for short distances must be at least 9 inches wide and 32 inches long — the marching shoe to measure 9 by 33 inches. The use of spikes of any sort is prohibited.

No artificial obstacles may be used for the start, no holes dug; nor is any assist from a coach or using someone else's foot as a brace permitted. The position for the start is drawn by lot. False starts (jumping the gun) are penalized by placing the offender one yard further behind the starting line for each false start. The runner, however, is disqualified after three such starts.

Once over lightly. These snowshoers take a difficult obstacle course with what looks like no effort at all. *Courtesy of Raoul Charbonneau*

On forced marches the runners must run with the body erect. Inclining the body forward at an unreasonable angle is not permitted, though arm movement is not restricted. Runners must finish the race on both snowshoes which must be still attached to the feet. If a snowshoe comes off during the race it must be put back on and retied before continuing. No help of any kind is permitted during any of the races or marches. (Cross-country ski racers take note of the differences.)

A runner in a distance race or forced march must be at least 12 feet in front of another runner before crossing into his opponent's lane. In the shorter races, 440 or less, he must stay in his own lane the entire race. In the 880, the runner must pass his opponents on the right except, if he leaves his own lane deliberately, another runner can use it to pass him on the inside. A runner may be disqualified for not trying to win and may not be permitted to race again for 6 months.

In the obstacle races (low hurdles) the hurdles must be 24 inches

Taking the high hurdles before a large crowd at the North American Championship Sled Dog Race meet in Fairbanks. *Alaska Travel Bureau*

in height and 30 inches wide. They must be mobile and placed 20 yards from the start and 20 yards from the finish line with the five additional hurdles spaced equally between. The runners must attempt to jump them straight on and must stay in their own lane. They cannot jump on the hurdles or upset them, nor can they jump them sideways by throwing both feet in the air at once.

## A Good Showing

It is interesting to match the times posted by the winners in international snowshoe races against foot race times for the same event. The following foot race times were taken from the results of a school boy track meet in the Greater Boston area, whereas the snowshoe times were taken from the official International Snowshoe Race Records as of 30 January 1974:

| event | track times | snowshoe times |
|-------|-------------|----------------|
| 100-yard dash | 10.9 seconds | 12.1 seconds |
| 220-yard dash | 23.2 seconds | 25.6 seconds |
| 440-yard dash | 51.7 seconds | 68.7 seconds |
| 880-yard dash | 2:03.0 minutes | 2:30.0 minutes |

Note that, as the distances get longer, the effect of the snowshoe's weight is more pronounced. To date there has not been enough publicity to attract enough attention from the outside world to make these snowshoe racers known outside their own circles. However, they are respected by their fellow performers and, after inspection of these close times, deserve the respect of all of us for the good showing they make with flapping snowshoes attached to their feet.

## Tips for Do-It-Yourself Racers

As with most competitive events for which there are governing bodies, the rules and specifications given here are subject to change. But, in general, they hit the highlights and are accurate. In any event, they certainly offer enough guidelines to give our readers all they need to try their own fun races without worrying too much about restrictions as to weight and shoe size. However, we do recommend preparing the race courses carefully by tracking and packing them firmly to ensure the same consistency of snow for everyone. Take care to remove any obstacles and hazards on or near the course. The measurements for distance should be taken three feet from the inside edge. For the distance races have adequate provisions for assistance to any sick or injured runner and a means to reach him quickly at any part of the course. Your guides or checkers can double up on this chore.

## Fun and Games

When any group of youngsters or oldsters get together on snowshoes they always seem to find ways to add a little spice and excitement to the outing. When this doesn't take the form of racing or just plain fooling around, it often takes the form of organized games. Here are some ideas for games that can be played on snowshoes:

## Compass Game

For the compass game, nine players and a referee tramp out

something rather resembling a wheel in the snow, the rim being about three snowshoes wide and the center area about ten yards across. Mark out a bulge or niche in the snow where North, South, West and East would be on the wheel. Then add bulges for the Northeast, Southeast, Southwest and Northwest. Connect them all to the center, or hub, like the spokes of a wheel. Station players at all the designated compass points and select one to be "it" or the "needle" in the center. Each person has to remember what compass point he is and what point the other players represent. The referee will call out two different points of the compass and the two players representing these points will try to exchange places at the same time the player in the middle tries to beat one of them to the vacated compass point. If "it" or the "needle " wins, the displaced player moves to the middle. The fun begins when, after a few shifts of position, the players forget their new positions and "it "starts to beat them to the spots. Any shortcuts between compass points is permissable, both for the needle and the points themselves. (If azimuths were used the approximate numbers called would be 360 and 180, 90 and 270, 45 and 135, or any combination thereof. This would really sharpen wits!)

In this game, everyone sharpens their sense of direction and has a good time as well. It can be an effective teaching device for the trip-minded youngster. Various changeoffs can be instituted such as having the players change place with the referee or having extra players fill in and change the circle completely to further confuse matters.

If the snow is over six inches deep, the entire circle may be tramped down to facilitate changing positions. However the fun will be even greater and the laughs louder if everyone is just left to flounder as they try to run through the deep snow.

## Fox and Geese

Fox and geese can be played on the same circle as the compass game but preferably before as once this lively game starts the wheel soon becomes unrecognizable due to the many criss-crossing tracks. In fox and geese, the fox stays in the middle while the geese run around the outside rim and dare him to catch them. He, the fox, must catch them between spokes on the rim, so there can't be too many spokes and enough distance between them to give the fox a chance.

## Dodge Ball

Dodge ball on snowshoes can be fun when played with a soft volleyball on a level area about the size of a basketball court. Establish the base lines and boundaries, mark the middle line and choose sides. Someone throws in the ball and then it's dodge and run for your life as each side tries to pick up the ball and then throw it to hit a man on the other side. If a player is hit, he drops out until the last survivor's team is declared the winner, or a time limit is set and the winner is determined by the number of players left on each side. No one is allowed to go outside the boundary line without being declared out. Only three steps can be taken before throwing the ball at another player. The ball may be passed behind the center line to players on the same side, and then thrown at an opposing player, but only twice before it must be thrown across the line, as in volleyball.

## A Rough One

A form of field hockey can be played on snowshoes if a colored ball is used and the playing surface is well tramped. The ball should be smaller than a volleyball but larger than a lacrosse ball — about the size of a softball would be ideal. In fact, color a softball and try it. Helmets may be desirable if the play becomes too fierce. Spills will be the order of the day so lethal stick swinging near an opponent who is down should be curtailed.

## Potatoes, Anyone?

For another kind of fun on snowshoes why not stage an old-fashioned potato race? For this event a basket is set in the center of a level snow-covered field or on the surface of a frozen lake. Potatoes, or similar objects, are then laid out at equal intervals in straight lines

Bridging the generation gap with a rousing game of baseball on snowshoes. *Alaska Travel Bureau*

extending away from the basket in the same way that the spokes radiate outwards from the hub of a wheel. Each snowshoe-shod contestant is assigned to a line of potatoes and stands with the tail of his snowshoes to the basket just sufficiently distant from the basket so as not to interfere with his competitors and yet close enough so no one has an advantage at the start. At the word "Go," all run out to the first potato in their lines, pick it up and return to drop it in the basket. The process is continued until the winner has gotten all of the potatoes from his line into the basket before anyone else. It soon becomes obvious that this game requires great skill in manipulating snowshoes in addition to considerable running ability.

## A Hard One

Or, try the ring race. Here the emphasis is laid on skill in getting into and out of snowshoe harnesses, as well as running on snowshoes and manipulating a ski pole. For this race, the contestants line up about ten yards behind their snowshoes which are laid out in pairs in a straight line pointing down the course. Each racer carries a single ski pole and, at the starting signal, must run forward, fasten on his snowshoes and then run ahead along the course. Midway down the course, along each racer's track, a ring with an interior diameter of two inches is laid in the snow. Each contestant must pick up the ring on the tip of the ski pole, holding the pole in one hand at the upper end only, and then continue along the course to the end where a pin is set vertically in the snow. This pin should have a diameter only slightly less than the inside of the ring. On arriving at the pin, the racer must deposit the ring over the pin still holding the pole in one hand at the upper end only. After the ring is on the pin, the contestants run back to where they put on their snowshoes, then take them off and run back to the starting line. In such an event, the snowshoe bindings should be of similar style so that one racer does not have an advantage over another.

## Running and Shooting

As we were talking over special events that might be performed on snowshoes we wondered whether some of our readers might like to experiment with an event which we call a snowshoe *biathlon*. The usual biathlon is an event in the winter Olympics which consists of skiing over a prepared course and shooting with rifles at fixed targets at predetermined points along the course. There are two main objectives in this competition: speed on skis and accuracy in shooting.

Our variation on this standard event is to replace skis with snowshoes and rifles with shotguns; then, instead of shooting at fixed targets, the contestants would fire at clay pigeons flung by the same device that is used on a trap shooting range. In our snowshoe biathlon, the contestants would be required to run on snowshoes along a marked course which has been carefully tramped out. The runners would carry a shotgun (probably the .410 caliber would be best) slung in the same manner as skiers carry a rifle. At one or more points along the course, catapults for slinging the clay targets into the air would be positioned. Scoring would be based on the same principles used for the regular biathlon; that is, misses in shooting would count as additions to the total elapsed time taken to cover the course.

Such a game should be of particular interest to snowshoeing hunters who are always anxious to improve their marksmanship and who might enjoy a little extra fun while at it. Since their quarry is almost always on the move, shooting at a moving target should prove especially intriguing and challenging.

These are only a few examples of races to run and games to play on snowshoes. No doubt you and your fellow snowshoers can think of many others to try — moments of sheer fun to add to all the other joys of snowshoeing.

# Making
# Your Own

Since the appearance of the first edition of *The Snowshoe Book* a number of people have asked us how they could learn to make their own snowshoes. As a result, we thought we would prepare a new chapter for this revised edition specifically on the technique and processes involved in the home manufacture of snowshoes.

To begin we should say that we undertake this chapter with some trepidation as we have not had a great deal of experience in this line. However, we have consulted with various skilled snowshoe craftsmen and have labored hard over several pairs of home-crafted snowshoes of our own, and now feel that the information we offer here should provide a good foundation for those who wish to take the time and pains to build snowshoes themselves.

Later in the chapter we will say something about putting together emergency snowshoes, or what we call "half-hour" snowshoes. This will expand the material given in the "Something Out of Nothing" section on pages 92 and 93 about expedient methods for hasty snowshoe construction. But for now let's get right to the more difficult matter at hand.

Making regular snowshoes will take considerably longer than half an hour. Warren Asa, writing on the subject in the Winter, 1971 issue of the *Hosteler* (magazine of the American Youth Hostels organization) says that it takes about ten hours of working time to make a pair of Michigan style snowshoes. While this may have been true for him, we found that making snowshoes from scratch requires quite a bit more time, and especially for the first pair when one has to add the time spent scouting up materials and tools. But, since we presume that anyone bent on making snowshoes is doing it for the sheer enjoyment of recreating an ancient craft, or as an experiment or challenge of some sort, the time element should not be that important. Just keep in mind that, if you do undertake making your own snowshoes, you will find it's a lengthy process from beginning to end and requires real dedication.

Let's assume that your first pair of snowshoes is to be made by the old method of using wood and rawhide (also known as *babiche*). The time to begin is in the spring just after the snow has left the ground. This will allow ample time to get them finished for the next winter's use.

Having set the rough time frame, we would suggest familiarizing yourself with the bill of materials and suggested tool and equipment list given here. These will give you a good idea of what you will need and a rough idea of the game plan.

---

### BILL OF MATERIALS FOR MAKING ONE PAIR OF OJIBWA STYLE SNOWSHOES
(approximately 10 1/2" wide by 52" long)

*Eight strips of air-dried white ash wood — 3/4" square by 54" long, tapered to 3/4" by 1/2" about 3" back from tips. Note: the extra pieces are in case of breakage during bending.*

*Four ash crossbars — two of them 1/4" by 1" by 10", two of them 1/4" by 1" by 7".*

*Thirteen yards of rawhide [babiche] strips 5' to 7' long by 3/8" wide to lace the center section. An additional thirteen yards of 1/4"-wide strips to lace the toe and heel sections.*

*Eight rivets and washers. 1/4" by 2".*

*One pint of polyurethane varnish.*

*Two bindings.*

### SUGGESTED LIST OF TOOLS AND EQUIPMENT FOR MAKING SNOWSHOES

*Axe, single-bitted.*
*Bow saw with 36" blade.*
*Two steel wedges, about 4 pounds each.*
*Maul for driving wedges.*
*Drawknife.*
*Drawshave or Jack plane.*
*Shaving horse [optional].*
*Six or more C-clamps.*
*Handsaw with crosscut teeth [optional].*
*Steaming rig.*
*Two bending jigs.*
*Cowhide from a full-grown beast.*
*Twelve-gallon or more capacity water tub.*
*Plenty of clean water.*
*Two pecks of dry hardwood ashes.*
*Burlap sacking and twine for bundling the hide.*
*Pole, sawhorses, etc. for "graining" the hide.*
*Drying rack for rawhide [optional: it can just hang over the pole].*
*Drill. 1/4" with nibs for cutting into wood.*
*Chisel with 1/2" bit.*
*Router [optional: to replace above two tools].*
*Sandpaper, medium and fine grit.*
*Circle for cutting rawhide into thongs [12" or 14" bowl: or a pair of compasses].*
*Waterproof marker.*
*Sharp knife set with gage for stripping out thongs.*
*Lacer's hook or needle.*
*Plenty of enthusiasm and patience.*

## The Dabiche

The first step is to get the rawhide. It is possible to buy rawhide ready to use, but if you plan to be a purist and start from scratch, you will want to get a fresh cowhide at a slaughterhouse. Cowhide makes excellent babiche and is comparatively easy to obtain. Ask the butcher to take some pains in removing the bits and pieces of flesh and fat from the inner surface as this material comes off much more easily when the hide is warm. The cost of such a skin will be about ten dollars but be prepared to find considerable variation. Sometimes you can even get one for no charge.

Other types of skins which have been used for snowshoe rawhide are: moose, caribou, deer, seal, beaver and bear. There is an interesting article by J.A. Burgesse on the subject of babiche and primitive snowshoe making in the March, 1941 issue of *The Beaver* (the journal of the Hudson's Bay Company). For greatest ease of operation, your rawhide preparation factory should be set up close to a good source of clean water; you will need a tub with at least a twelve-gallon capacity. The first step is to put the green cowhide in the tub, filling the tub with enough water to cover the hide completely. Weight the hide with stones to keep it under the surface of the water. Cover the tub to keep out inquisitive animals and let the hide soak for a couple of days.

## The Frame Stock

While the hide soaks is the time to procure the wood for the frames. The authors happen to be in the enviable position of having ample woodlands at our disposal but we realize that most people cannot just go out in the forest, select a prime tree and cut it. If you do not have access to your own woods, there are several alternatives open. The necessary wood can be purchased or arrangements can be made with a forest owner. Let's assume you can make proper arrangements with a woodlot owner; the next step is a pleasant excursion to look for a "Snowshoe Tree."

## The "Snowshoe Tree"

All of the following trees (and probably others we have not heard of) have been used for making snowshoe frames:

Quaking Aspen (Populus tremuloides)
Paper Birch (Betula papyrifera)
Yellow Birch (Betula alleghaniensis)
American Elm (Ulmus americana)
Slippery Elm (Ulmus rubra)
Shagbark Hickory (Carya ovata)
Red Maple (Acer rubrum)
Sugar Maple (Acer saccharum)
Northern Red Oak (Quercus rubra)
Black Spruce (Picea mariana)
Red Spruce (Picea rubens)
White Spruce (Picea glauca)
Black Willow (Salix nigra)

However, the best snowshoe frames are made from the wood of the ash tree. Of the sixteen varieties of ash trees, five may be considered suitable for snowshoe making. These are the white, black, green, blue, and Oregon ash. The latter occurs naturally only in the states of Washington, Oregon and California and in the Province of British Columbia. White ash (Fraxinus americana) and black ash (Fraxinus nigra) are fairly common in northeastern United States and around the Great Lakes district; also in the southeastern Canadian provinces.

Most skilled snowshoe makers would agree that the white ash is the "Lord of the Snowshoe Trees" as the wood is very tough, shock resistant, and relatively easy to bend after it has been steamed. White ash is sometimes called Biltmore ash. Look for the white ash on upland sites where the soil is well drained. It seldom grows in pure stands and is most often found growing amongst the Eastern White Pine, Northern Red Oak, White Oak, Sugar Maple, Red Maple, Yellow Birch, American Beech, Black Cherry, American Basswood, Eastern Hemlock, American Elm and Yellow Poplar.

Black ash is also much used for snowshoe frames, particularly

Parts of the ash tree.

in Wisconsin and Minnesota. This tree can tolerate wetter growing conditions. It is also called brown, basket, hoop, swamp, and water ash.

As the diagram shows, the bark of the ash is gray with rather deep furrows separated by narrow, interlacing ridges. The leaves are compound. If you are looking for ash trees before the leaves have appeared, check the branches. Characteristically, the branches grow exactly opposite each other almost at right angles from the stem making the sign of the cross. For those who might need a short course in tree identification we can certainly recommend the little booklet prepared by the U.S. Forest Service: *Important Trees of Eastern Forests and Trees of North America: A Golden Field Guide* by C. Frank Brockman. It has fine illustrations and is easy to use.

Any tree that's to be used for making snowshoe frames must be straight, free from imperfections and with no branches to a height of about fifteen or twenty feet. The bark can sometimes be used as an indicator of whether or not the wood is straight-grained. If the furrowed bark on the trees runs in vertical lines evenly the chances are good that the wood will split with a minimum of twisting. The diameter of the tree near the base should be six to ten inches. Anything much larger will be awkward to handle, especially as most people don't own log skidding equipment.

## Felling

After locating and obtaining permission to take the snowshoe tree, the next step is to cut it down. In cutting a tree it is much better for two people to work together. Working this way makes it both easier and safer.

Before beginning the cut it is wise to check the lean of the tree. This will effect the line of fall and your decision as to where best to fell the tree. Obviously, if a tree leans one way or another one has to account for this in planning where to fell it, to avoid binding the saw in the cut and other complications.

Once the line of fall is determined, cut a notch in the tree near the base on the side where you wish the tree to fall. The notch, or undercut, should be as near horizontal as possible and about one quarter way through the tree. The best way to start the notch is to make one cut for the bottom edge with the saw and then chop out the rest of the notch, or scarf, with the axe.

Begin the next saw cut, or backcut, on the side of the tree opposite the notch and just slightly above the lower edge of the scarf. A bow saw, when used by two persons pulling alternately, works very nicely for this. Stand clear of the tree as it is about to fall and watch above for flying limbs, often called "widow-makers" and with good reason. A word to the wise: the expert felling of trees is an art; if you are a beginner in this field, a few minutes spent with a good woodsman's manual (for instance, the "Felling" chapter in Rockwell Stephen's *One Man's Forest*) might save you a lot of headaches.

Once the tree is down, using the axe, cut off all the limbs close to the trunk of the tree. Be sure to save as much of this limb wood as possible since it can be used later to fire up the steaming apparatus. Wood of the ash tree makes a nice hot fire and burns well even when green.

## "Getting Out" the Stock

Commercial snowshoe makers use sawed lumber in getting out frame stock, but the home snowshoe maker will probably find that it is best to work the wood to correct size by first sawing off the proper length bolts, then by splitting, hewing, and shaving. Ash splits very nicely and all that will be needed for this is a couple of steel wedges and a maul to drive them with. (Don't be tempted to use the head of the axe to drive wedges — it's very hard on the axe.)

### Cutting the Bolts

Before deciding how long to cut the rough bolts to be used for the frames from the main log, you must have determined which type of snowshoe you wish to make. Refer back to pages 29 through 34 for a description of several popular models. The table below indicates how long to cut the bolts for five snowshoe styles and allows for a bit extra for trimming the ends later.

| Snowshoe | Projected size | Length of bolt |
|---|---|---|
| Green Mtn. Bearpaw | 10" x 36" | should be 87" |
| Standard Bearpaw | 12" x 30" | should be 80" |
| Michigan | 12" x 42" | should be 94" |
| Alaskan Trail | 10" x 56" | should be 119" |
| Ojibwa | 10" x 48" | should be 54" |

If you wish to make snowshoes other than the styles given in the table you will need to obtain a snowshoe to use as a pattern. To find the correct length for the unbent frame just measure around the perimeter of the model snowshoe with a tape ruler and add an inch or so.

Once the bolts are cut is a good time to check the sawed ends to determine the number of annual growth rings. The best ash wood for making snowshoe frames has from twelve to fifteen annual growth rings per inch. If there are more, the frames will be difficult to bend and will not be as strong.

## Splitting

When the bolt has been sawed to the correct length and checked for suitability, the bolt is split. To do this, place one of the wedges *exactly* in the center of the sawed off end. To get the best results the split should begin at the end of the bolt that was nearest the top of the tree. Drive the wedge in with the maul; in most cases the bolt of ash wood will split cleanly with just one wedge needed. If the split is not completed with the first wedge, a second can be placed along the crack to finish the job; or in many cases a considered blow with the axe will accomplish the same results. After the bolt has been split, check the split surface for straightness of grain. This should not diverge more than one inch in every fifteen inches.

Next is a good time to peel off the bark. If you are doing this work in the springtime you will find that the bark peels off readily. At other times of the year it may be necessary to use a drawknife to get the bark off. The bark must go as it is of no use at all, except possibly as fuel when it is dry. With the bark off, you can see the outer surface of the sapwood and can examine it closely for signs of small knots that might have been covered by the bark.

Using the drawknife to strip
the bark from the bolt.

Cut and split several bolts of wood in this manner, checking each for the qualities mentioned above. Select out the best of the split halves and quarter them, using the wedge and maul as before. A bolt that is about ten inches in diameter can be split once again thus giving eight pieces. It is much more difficult to get good splits from bolts that are smaller in diameter so only split those into quarters.

All of this work can be done right where the tree was cut. Reducing the size of the pieces to be carried back to the workshop eases the chore. A four-foot long bolt of freshly cut white ash six inches in diameter at the large end weighs in at fifty pounds or so. Before leaving the area, salvage as much of the tree as possible to use as firewood; then assemble the materials gathered thus far at the place where you will finish shaving the frames down to size and where the steaming and bending will be done.

## Hewing

The next step is to hew the frame stock down to size — in this case, a strip about an inch and a half wide by an inch and a half high. When the wood is newly cut, we have found it works best to use a very sharp axe. Working around the sapwood, carefully hew off most of the heartwood to roughly shape the frame stock. This can be done by eye, or if you don't trust your eye, use a straightedge to check the work from time to time. Hew slowly and deliberately as a false stroke with the axe can ruin the whole job. Watch for the way the grain of the wood runs and always hew or shave with the grain, not against it. Never cut into the sapwood as this is the most valuable part of the stick and will form the outer edge of the snowshoe frame.

Shorter sticks can be hewed by holding the pieces in an upright position on a chopping block with one hand while striking the axe with the other. Hold the axe handle about midway. Longer pieces will need to be placed horizontally on a couple of blocks of wood laid on the ground with one end of the stick resting against a firm surface to keep it from slipping back each time the axe strikes. This work can be done in a kneeling position. If you have never done much work with an axe before you will come to appreciate the skills of the old-time woodsman.

Using an axe to hew and shape a piece of frame stock while a good working steamer gets hot in the foreground. Normally, since the hewed frame stock must dry before using, these steps would not occur concurrently. *Bridge Hill Studio photo.*

### Shaving

Once the hewing is done the frame stock will have to be shaved down to finish size by using first a drawknife and then a drawshave. The drawknife is a two-handled tool with a single beveled cutting edge running between the handles at right angles and on the same plane (see diagram). It is worked by pulling it towards the operator while the material is clamped to a bench.

There is a special kind of bench for this work called a shaving horse. It is described in Alex W. Bealer's *Old Ways of Working Wood* (Barre Publishers, 1972). There is also a picture of a shaving horse and other valuable information on the old crafts in *The Foxfire Book* (Doubleday Anchor Books, 1972). However, since we assume that most people attempting to make snowshoes will not wish to go to the extra work of making a shaving horse, we advise that the work simply be clamped to a bench while being shaved. C-clamps or carpenters' hand screws can be used for this. The clamps will also be needed later to hold the bent frames on the jigs after they have been steamed.

When the frame stock has been shaved down to a little over three-quarters by three-quarters inches, finish the shaving to a final dimension of three-quarter-inches square with the drawshave or a jack or block plane. A drawshave (also see diagram) is similar to a drawknife except that its blade projects through a slot in the body of the tool so that a shaving of controlled thickness can be taken off. As with a plane, the thickness of the shaving can be regulated by moving the blade in or out and clamping it in the desired position. With shaving as with hewing, never cut into the sapwood. Any slight imperfections there can be smoothed off later after the frame has been steamed and bent.

All snowshoe frames require that additional wood be shaved out to facilitate bending. The Ojibwa frame which is in two pieces

Shaping and shaving the frame stock with a drawshade.

for each snowshoe is tapered smoothly down to a half inch by three quarters of an inch at either end where the toe and tail are fixed together. Other styles have some wood removed from the inner edge at the place where the toe bend comes. Additionally, bearpaw styles are tapered down at the tail so that when bent the tail portion of the frame will be of equal width throughout where the ends overlap. Here again consult the diagram of your chosen snowshoe design, or better still, the real thing.

### Drying

Make up enough finished stock to have extra pieces on hand at the time the frames are bent as about one in five break when the wood is forced into the unnatural position of a snowshoe frame. When you have sufficient stock ready, the pieces should be put aside in a cool, dry place to season in the air. Some snowshoe makers advise going right ahead with the steaming and bending, but we think it is best to allow the stock to air dry. A month will bring the wood down to about an ideal twenty per cent moisture content. Wood set aside to dry should be laid horizontally with the longer pieces supported in the middle to avoid sagging. Allow plenty of room for air circulation by putting thin strips of wood crosswise between layers.

We figure that the work involved in getting this much of the job done — the cutting, splitting, hewing and shaping — will take a full day under ideal conditions and more likely two or three days, and this assuming that only one or two pair of snowshoes are going to be made.

## Back to the Babiche

The interlude while the shaped frame stock dries can be used to advantage to finish the babiche, to make up the bending jigs, and to put together some sort of steam generating apparatus.

If the hide was put to soak in clear water as suggested earlier, it should be fully softened and ready for the next step after two or three days. When ready, pull the hide out of the tub and lay it flat on the ground with the flesh side up. Using a sharp knife, *carefully* cut loose any remaining bits of fat and meat. Then trim off the edges of the hides so that it is roughly rectangular. This will mean cutting off the portions which formerly covered the legs, and the soft, thin belly section.

Once the hide is trimmed, turn the hide over so the hair side is up and cover the hair liberally with hardwood ashes. Pour enough water on the ashes to make a thick paste and work it into the hair thoroughly with a stick. Don't use your hands for this as the caustic action released by wood ashes being moistened with water can be very hard on your skin. Roll up the hide with the hair side in and tie the bundle up tightly. Put it in a damp, cool place, perhaps on the earthen floor of a cellar. Cover it with wet burlap and let it stay there for three or four days. Be prepared for a struggle — a sopping wet cowhide at this stage will weigh close to sixty pounds.

## Making the Jig

While the lye in the ashes is loosening the hair from the hide is a good time to be thinking about the design of the bending jig and planning the steam generator for softening the wood.

The easiest sort of jig to make would be the type for flat bearpaw snowshoes with no upturn at the toes (see diagram). An old plank of softwood two inches thick by twelve inches wide and at least five feet long will serve the purpose. Take the snowshoe you intend to duplicate and cut out a cardboard pattern to fit the inside of the frame; or use the snowshoe itself as the pattern. Hold the pattern or the snowshoe on the plank, and using a soft lead pencil, scribe along the edge of the pattern or the *inside* edge of the snowshoe frame so that the outline is transferred to the plank. Using a handsaw you can cut off most of the surplus wood: then finish the job by hewing with the axe, drawknife and block plane until the entire jig has a smooth outline.

The next step is to prepare the holes for the clamps. To do this, find some cast-off pieces of iron waterpipe with at least a one-inch

A bearpaw frame on its jig with the clamps in place.

inside diameter; then, with a hacksaw cut off about twenty-four lengths of the same thickness as the bending jig. The reason for the pipe is that it acts as reinforcement when the clamps are tightened.

Next, select a wood-boring auger the correct size to cut a hole equal to the outside diameter of the iron pipe. Bore a number of holes about one and one half inches in from the edge of the bending jig. The holes should be placed where there will be the most bending tension. The primary hole will be at the front, or toe, end of the jig. Fit the pieces of iron pipe into the holes, securing them in place with glue if they are a bit loose. Normally, one jig is required for each snowshoe you plan to make. We have considered trying to bend a *pair* of flat bearpaw snowshoes on a single jig but haven't gotten around to doing this yet.

## Jig Variations

Different jigs are necessary for bending snowshoes with upturn at the toes. These require a shaped block to hold the bent toe plus the right amount of upturn. A variation on the hole and clamp variety of jig we have described would be a jig with blocks of wood nailed and glued in place along the inner outline of the snowshoe pattern. Yet another variation would be a jig made of a plank with the toe end shaped to give the right amount of upturn for Ojibwa style snowshoes (see diagram). A piece of board is affixed to the

The jig for an Ojibwa snowshoe with the frame in place. Note the additional piece affixed to the front to hold the tip in position while it dries.

underside of the jig with a hole exactly in the center of this board large enough to receive the joined tips of this style. And two spreaders are nailed to the jig at about the place where the front and rear crossbars will later be placed. This is very well described in Ben Hunt's *Big Indian Craft Book* (Bruce Publishing Company, 1945).

## Once Again the Babiche

### Cleaning

With the jig completed, attention can be turned back to the babiche. Three or four days of curing should loosen the hair from the hide enough so it can be scraped off. Open the bundle and try a section. If the hair is still tight add some more ashes and water and bundle the skin up again for another day or so. After the hair has loosened sufficiently take the bundle outside, open it up and rinse off the wood ashes, as well as any hair that is willing to come along. A good stream of water from a hose is just right to thoroughly cleanse the hide. When thoroughly rinsed hang the hide over a long pole suspended between two sawhorses.

## Graining

The next step is called "graining." For this you can use the same drawknife that was used for shaving the wood off the snowshoe frames, only with a big difference. This time the back, blunt edge of the drawknife is used and instead of pulling it towards you, you push it away from you over the hide against the direction of the hair — this to clean off the hair and the scarf skin or epidermis. This job takes lots of elbow grease. There are special tools made for graining babiche, but we think the drawknife will work well enough for only one or two hides. Scrape both sides of the skin carefully, rinsing it from time to time to keep it moist and to wash off the debris.

A cold, wet and rainy day is just the time for this sort of a job. Wear a pair of rubber boots and waterproof overalls so you can sit astraddle the pole and hold the hide to keep it from slipping away as you scrape, scrape, scrape. If you get tired just put the hide back in the tub and cover it with fresh water until you have recovered your energy for another scraping bout. This is the type of work that is best to do in early spring before the weather gets warm enough to turn the hide putrid and make your job even more difficult.

## Drying

When the scraping sessions are finished, you will need a rack for drying the hide. For this, use four poles lashed tightly together at each corner to form a rectangle about six inches larger than the size of the hide. Allow two of the poles to be long enough to keep the frame well away from the ground when the drying begins. When the hide has been scraped smooth and clean on both sides lay it on the ground and cut a series of slots near the edge on all four sides and about eight to ten inches apart. Lash the hide to the drying frame so that it is quite tight and put the frame on end in a shady place, perhaps against a building or some trees, where the breeze can blow on it to dry it thoroughly. If a spot can be found out of the reach of inquiring animals so much the better.

Check the lashing from time to time and tighten or loosen it as may he required. Rather soon it will be dry and hard as a board and you will see how babiche in this state could have been very effective when used by warring Indians as a shield to deflect enemy arrows. As long as the hide remains dry it will last indefinitely and could be stored in any sheltered place out of the reach of gnawing rodents.

## The Steamer

The steam generator is the next order of business. We have used an old cast-iron pig-feeding trough covered with a section of old sheet-iron roofing with success. The trough, where the frame stock will be steamed, is supported on stones and a fire built under and around it to bring the water in the trough to a boil. Another possibility would be to get an old water heater tank at the dump. Take it to someone who has oxy-acetylene gas cutting and welding equipment. Have one end cut off square with the cutting torch and then have the tank cut in half lengthwise. The cut ends welded together will provide a steaming tank about ten feet long.

Mr. Richard L. Floyd of Ely, Minnesota, who has made many pairs of snowshoes as a hobby, says that his steaming equipment is ". . . simply a ten foot length of six inch pipe with one end welded shut. I elevate the open end about five feet off the ground, fill the pipe with water, light a fire under the closed end and I'm in business." If you can tap a steam line conveniently you could direct the steam into a length of stove pipe which has the open end stuffed loosely with rags. We have even thought that snowshoe frames could be steamed on top of a maple syrup evaporator during the sugaring season. There are many possibilities that could be improvised out of available materials. The objective in any case is to thoroughly impregnate the wood with plenty of moist heat.

## Fabricating the Frames

## Bending

The moment of truth comes on steaming and bending day when likely you will find that some of the labor you expended on hewing and shaving the frame stock was for naught. Often some of the wood breaks while being bent so be prepared for some disappointments.

First, fire up your steamer. Put the frame stock itself right in the tank and then keep the apparatus going full tilt for at least two hours before trying to bend any of the stock. Being careful to use heavy gloves when taking the frame stock out of the steam chest, try each piece for "bendability." When a piece seems supple enough, clamp it to the jig made for it at the point where the toe of the snowshoe will be, then bend the rest of it right around and clamp as necessary. (Obviously, this procedure changes to accommodate the different snowshoe patterns; the bearpaw requiring one solid piece of stock bent from the middle, the Ojibwa two separate pieces, etc.) Work quickly. It's good to have a helper at this stage.

In several of the snowshoe factories we have visited we have noticed that the workers put a band of flexible metal strapping on the tip section with gripper pliers to give some reinforcement to that critical point when the bend is made.

Frames bent and clamped to the jigs should be left in place for at least a week; then they may be removed and allowed to dry further for two weeks more. During this second drying stage it will be important to place some wooden spreaders inside the frame to help hold the shape. If, by this time, the season has moved along into summer you might want to put the frames in the attic where they will dry all the more quickly up under the roof.

## Fitting the Cross Bars

While the frames dry would be a good time to whittle out the crossbars. Each pair of the snowshoe styles we have been discussing requires a total of four crossbars; these can be made out of the same

Here two well-steamed pieces of frame stock are being bent to fit an Ojibwa jig. Note how the two pieces of the tip are held tight by the clamp and how the center pieces are fitted around the stretchers. *Bridge Hill Studio photos.*

wood the frame stock came from. Each crossbar will be about one and one-half inches wide by one-quarter inch thick with the length to be determined by just where the crossbar fits on the frame.

Fitting in the crossbars can be done in several ways. If you are using a finished snowshoe for a model, you can measure the model and use those measurements to find the location for the crossbars on the new snowshoes. Another method is to balance the new frame horizontally across a straightedge and then lay on the crossbars in their approximate positions about fifteen to seventeen inches apart. Move them until the snowshoe frame is slightly tail-heavy and mark the location of the crossbars in the frame with a pencil. This will indicate where the mortices are to be cut in.

Professional snowshoe makers put the mortices (a mortice, by the way, is nothing but a cabinetmaker's term for a slot) in with a power tool called a router. The same thing can be done with a hand drill and a chisel. Whether a power router is used or hand tools, the mortices should be carefully cut in to the dimension of one inch long, one-quarter inch deep by one-quarter inch wide. The ends of the crossbars can then be very carefully shaved down to fit the mortices.

Before the crossbars are put in place the ends of the frames are secured either with rivets or rawhide. The Ojibwa snowshoes have to be joined at both toes and tails while, as we have seen, the other models are only joined at the tails. In either case, holes will have to be made to receive rivets or rawhide (see diagram). The same quarter-inch drill that was used to make the mortices can do this job too. After the frames have been joined together, they can be sprung apart slightly and the crossbars slipped in place. No glue is needed.

This diagram shows where the two pieces making the tip and tail of the Ojibwa frame should be riveted together, as well as where to place the crossbars and where to drill the holes for the toe and heel lacing. The toe crossbar should be 10 inches wide, while the heel crossbar should be 7 inches. Note that the crossbars are also drilled for lacing holes.

## Drilling the Lace Holes

Before you put the drill away plan to make the holes to be used for lacing the toe and heel sections. At this point, rather than try to deal with all the various, and rather complex, lacing patterns possible, we'll restrict our explanation to one type of snowshoe, the Ojibwa. The diagrams show very clearly where the holes are to be drilled. When drilling the holes clamp a piece of softwood to the under side directly below where the drill enters. This will avoid unwanted splintering. A fine touch would be to countersink each hole slightly. Beyond this, Mr. Floyd advises cutting a groove between holes as added protection to the lacing of the toe and heel sections. The final step before the lacing begins is to sand down any imperfections on the frame and carefully to take off all sharp edges that might chafe the lacing.

## The Lacing

To prepare the dried babiche for cutting into lacing thongs first smooth it with sandpaper or pumice stone. Then, check the dry rawhide over for uneven spots and note where the hide is of best quality. Turn a twelve- or fourteen-inch mixing bowl upside down over the good spots on the hide and trace a circle with an indelible marker around every place where the hide can be used.

At this point, put the hide back in warm water to soak again for a while. Even with this soaking the hide will likely still be stiff, you will probably have to cover it with burlap or other rags soaked in warm water to soften it enough to cut around the circles. After cutting, soak the circular sections a bit more until they are quite flexible, but not too soft to slice out the lacing material.

Lacing material three-eighths of an inch wide is best for center section lacing. A quarter of an inch or slightly less is good for toe and heel lacing. You will find that the lacing shrinks a bit on drying. It shrinks both in width, thickness and length. There is also considerable variation in the hide thickness depending on where it had been on the animal. Skin on the back is much thicker than belly hide. While the latter would be alright for lacing toe and heel sections, it would be far too flimsy for lacing the center sections. Keep these things in mind while cutting up your babiche and sorting out the lacing thongs.

## Cutting the Thongs

A rather simple way of making the lacing thongs is to drive a small nail part way into the work bench and press the tip of a *very sharp* knife into the bench three-eighths of an inch away from the nail with the blade slanting just slightly backwards.

Then, with another sharp knife cut along the circumference of a circle of babiche to provide a short starting strip. Fit this strip between the knife blade and the nail on the bench and then, by pulling on the starter strip, force the uncut hide against the cutting edge of the knife to get fairly long strips of lacing material as the circular piece of hide goes round and round until the center is reached. Aim for strips as long as possible.

To make the narrower quarter-inch strips, just set the knife closer to the nail and start again. It takes a bit of practice to get just the right slant on the knife blade to make the lacing you want, but once things are set up properly it all goes rather quickly. If you intend to begin weaving the pattern on the frames right away, throw the newly cut strips of lacing into a pail of water; otherwise, you can let the lacing dry up again for storage.

## Lacing the Shoes

The best way to learn to lace snowshoes would be as an apprentice to a master lacer. Lacking that opportunity the next best way is to work from the diagrams that Grace Brigham has drawn for this chapter. She has simplified the traditional Ojibwa pattern somewhat to make the lacing easier.

We think it is easier to lace with babiche than with the new synthetics. When rawhide is wet it's very flexible and easy to cut. Lacing with rawhide is best done with lengths of from five to seven feet, splicing lengths together as needed.

## Splicing

To make a splice in rawhide, cut a half-inch slit lengthwise of the thong in use, beginning the slit about a quarter-inch back from the end. Cut a corresponding slit in the thong which will be attached. Pass the end of the first piece through the slit in the piece to be attached and then draw the loose end of the new thong through the slit in the one being spliced into. One does not need too much tension; just draw it up rather snug. Later, when the rawhide dries, it will shrink nice and tight.

## Lacing Aids

Some professional lacers have a special clamp to hold the snowshoe steady while they are working. Others grip the frame between the body and one arm but this takes a good deal of agility. We suggest that the frame be clamped to a firm surface at an angle of about seventy degrees thereby leaving both hands free. A convenient lacing tool is shaped like an oversized crochet hook. Some Indians use a bone needle with a hole in the middle and a blunt point at either end. These are great aids, with the lacing hook being easier to learn to use than the needle.

## The Strategy

The lacing for the center section is done first. It is started on the left hand side of the frame about four and one-half inches down from the crossbar. The master or toe cord is the first part to be done. To complete the center section lacing, follow the diagrams. Any splicing in the center section should be done at the frame.

Working from upper left to lower right, and using 33 feet of 3/8th-inch cord, follow these diagrams to lace the center section of an Ojibwa snowshoe. It looks complicated but with patience and care this pattern can be mastered.

LACING AN OJIBWA SNOWSHOE

At top: the final tie-off pattern for the Ojibwa lacing pattern shown at left. At right: the pattern for the toe and heel sections of the Ojibwa is identical. Use 8 feet of 1/4-inch cord for each.

When the center section has been laced, it is set aside to dry overnight. The next day a reinforcing thong of babiche is wound around the toe or master cord and sometimes around the lengths that form the sides of the toe hole.

It doesn't matter in which order the toe and heel sections are laced. In order to help thread the babiche through the holes in the frame it is handy to take a piece of wire and double it over the end of the thong. Splices in toe and heel sections are not made at the frame. Here again follow the diagrams.

Let the completely laced snowshoes dry thoroughly and then give them a good coat of polyurethane varnish. The only thing left to do then is to make up some bindings. Some suggested binding patterns are given on pages 53 through 61. Rawhide for bindings can be made flexible by rubbing plenty of neatsfoot oil into the thongs when they are dry and then drawing the thongs back and forth over the edge of a board to make them supple.

## Alternative Laces

We have gone to some length to explain as much as we could about preparing babiche so that those who wished to could make their own snowshoes as much along traditional lines as possible.

The finished snowshoe.

However, we realize that some may wish to skip the rawhide step completely. Good lacing material can be purchased at any local hardware store in the form of one-eighth inch halyard weave nylon cord. This can be used very well to lace all three of the snowshoe sections; toe and heel as well as center section. In using nylon cord keep plenty of tension on it while lacing and keep splices or knots to a minimum. Another substitute for babiche is the Neoprene lacing that has become very popular for snowshoes. Some snowshoe manufacturers sell this in thirteen-yard strips.

Yet another substitute for rawhide is the metal mesh called hardware cloth. Some years ago Popular Mechanics magazine published an article giving complete directions for using this cloth for snowshoes. A reprint of this article can be purchased from them for $1.10 by sending an order to: Popular Mechanics, Dept. CO, Box 1014, Radio City, New York, 10019.

## Using a Kit

For budding snowshoe makers who would prefer not to start from scratch, there are kits available on the market. They come complete with all components, including Neoprene strands for lacing, and with full directions for assembly. These kits are relatively new and we have not yet had a chance to evaluate them. We understand they are almost as expensive as finished snowshoes, but for those who enjoy putting things together, they might be a good possibility. For those that are interested, Vermont Tubbs and Black Forest Enterprises are among the companies that offer these kits.

## "Half-Hour" Snowshoes

As we indicated at the start, we do not want to close this new chapter on making your own snowshoes without some reference to what we call "half-hour" snowshoes. These are the type that might be used in an emergency situation and are not intended for long trips.

In the "Something out of Nothing" section on pages 92 and 93 we mentioned some facts about expedient methods for hasty snowshoe construction. Since that section was written we have had the experience of a class in outdoor education composed of women students who actually made and used these simple snowshoes as part of their training. We call them "half-hour" snowshoes because this is how long it took these students to make them.

For each snowshoe these students broke off five to seven branches of the Jack Pine, selecting those branches with the most needles, each branch being about three feet long. Three branches were used for the base with the butts forming the toe of the snowshoe and the tips the tail. Since there is a natural bend to the limbs this could be used to advantage to create a slight upturn to the snowshoes making them less likely to dig into the snow when worn. In addition to the three or four branches needed for the base of each snowshoe, a couple were added to form a rough pocket for the foot which was tied into this pocket in a position to make the snowshoe slightly tail heavy. The branches were tightly banded together with wire or twine. Anyone could follow this simple procedure to make emergency snowshoes. A good style of binding to use would be the Alaskan type shown on page 54.

The user might still find it better to take a turn around the tips, over the butt ends of the branches, and to pull back with some slight tension to create a bit more upturn. This would give the effect of trail-type snowshoes which are more effective in deep snow. This type of emergency equipment will give good service for trips of four to five miles. They have about half the flotation qualities of regular snowshoes.

Jack Pine (Pinus banksiana), the tree used for making the 'half-hour' snowshoes described above, is quite a common tree in Canada and in the northernmost United States. Branches of other evergreen trees are also suitable. A prime quality is needed with plenty of needles to help provide good flotation in deep, soft snow.

The students, in their case, were careful to use trees on college land and avoid impairing the future growth of any tree. One might not be able to be quite so conscientious in an emergency situation but thought should be given to the proper conservation of growing things whenever possible. The time has passed when we can just go out into the forest and cut indiscriminately.

For those interested in more information along this line, William H. Bradfield has spent quite a bit of time studying emergency-type snowshoes. His article on the subject in the November, 1973 issue of *Field and Stream* magazine is worth reading. As we have done, he also cautions prudence in the use of the woodlands for gathering materials to make this type of snowshoe.

# SNOWSHOE MAKERS

The following is a partial list of snowshoe and snowshoe equipment makers in the United States and Canada. It is not intended as a complete list but merely as an up-to-date indication of the general distribution of these craftsmen in North America and as a good source of information about snowshoes. Snowshoes may also be bought and inquired about through the many excellent sporting goods stores and mail order houses in both countries.

## U.S.A.

Black Forest Enterprises
P.O. Box 1007
Nevada City, California 95959

Iverson's Snowshoes
Shingleton, Michigan 49884

JDK Sports, Inc.
P.O. Box 1014
Boulder, Colorado 80302

Snocraft Division
Garland Manufacturing Co.
53 Water Street - Box 71
Saco, Maine 04072

Sportsmen Products
P.O. Box 1082
Boulder, Colorado 80302

Trappe of Aspen
Division of Woodstream Corp.
Lititz, Pennsylvania 17543

Vermont Tubbs, Inc.
18 Elm Street
Wallingford, Vermont 05773

Floyd Westover
Meco, Box 63, R.D.1
Gloversville, New York 12078

## CANADA

Aigle Noir, Enr.
42 De La Passerelle
Loretteville, Province of Quebec

Avery & Sons
Whitney, Ontario

Bastien Brothers, Inc.
136 Est, Des Erables
St.-Emile, Province of Quebec

Bastien Manufacturing, Enr.
Village des Hurons,
Province of Quebec

Big Chief Manufacturing Reg'd
P.O. Box 176
Loretteville, Province of Quebec

Canadian Lacrosse
  Manufacturing
2440 Bonin Street
Sherbrooke, Province of Quebec

Chestnut Canoe Co., Ltd.
P.O. Box 85
Fredericton, New Brunswick

Faber & Company
P.O. Box 100
Loretteville, Province of Quebec

Magline of Canada
Highway 17
P.O. Box 219
Renfrew, Ontario

Picard & Frère Enrg.
Village des Hurons,
Province of Quebec

Sher-Craft
1511 Cabana Street
Sherbrooke, Province of Quebec

# FOR FURTHER READING

Although there are few books devoted completely to snowshoes and snowshoeing, there is a substantial literature on the subject, primarily in periodicals. For example, *Appalachia* — published 13 times a year by the Appalachian Mountain Club (5 Joy Street, Boston, Massachusetts) — is a fine resource. The *Beaver* — published quarterly by the Hudson's Bay Company (Hudson's Bay House, Winnipeg 1, Canada) — is another good source. Below is a short but selective list of reading on snowshoeing that we have particularly enjoyed.

American Alpine Club, *Accidents in North American Mountaineering, Including Canada and the United States.* New York, N.Y., Yearly. (Write 113 East 90th Street.)

Becket, Hugh W., *The Montreal Snow Shoe Club*, Becket Bros., Montreal, 1882

Brockman, C. Frank, *Important Trees of Eastern Forests and Trees of North America: A Golden Field Guide.* U.S. Forest Service.

Danielson, John, *Winter Hiking and Camping*, Adirondack Mountain Club.

Davidson, Daniel S., *Snowshoes: memoirs of the American Philosophical Society*, v. 6, 1937. American Philosophical Society, Philadelphia, 1937.

Drummond, Thomas, *The Canadian Snowshoe.* J. Hope, Ottawa, 1916.

Evans, Robert Jay, "Winter Climb in New Hampshire," *Summit*, November, 1959.

Gilman, Roger B., "Snowshoes," *Appalachia*, December, 1969.

Kjellstrom, Bjorn, *Be Expert with Map and Compass.* American Orienteering Service, LaPorte, Indiana, 1967. (Note: this book does not deal with snowshoes, but it does have excellent instructions for those who would like to try bushwhacking on snowshoes.)

Mellor, Malcolm, *Avalanches.* Cold Regions Research & Engineering Laboratory, Hanover, N.H.

Prater, Gene, *Snowshoe Hikes in the Cascades and Olympics.* The Mountaineers, Seattle, 1969. (Write P.O. Box 122.)

————— , "Techniques of Mountain Snowshoeing," *Summit,* December, 1970.

U.S. Dept. of Agriculture, "The Snowy Torrents," Avalanche Accidents in the United States, 1910-1966. Washington, D.C., 1967.

# INDEX

Alaskan (snowshoe style), 32–33, 47, 133; *ill.*, 32
Aleuts, 38
Algonquin (snowshoe style), 31; *ill.*, 32
Aluminum snowshoes, 35–36, 45
American Snowshoe Union, 20–21
Animal tracks, 86–89; *ill.*, 86, 87, 89
Anorak, 65–66
Army binding, 50–52, 69; *ill.* 51, 52
Avalanches, 96–107; *ill.* 101, 102

Babiche, 44, 129, 138–139, 141–143
See also Lacing, Lacing patterns
Balata binding, 51–52; *ill.* 52
Battle on snowshoes, 14
Bearpaw (snowshoe style), 29, 32, 47, 133; *ill.* 30, 32, 35, 140
Beavertail (snowshoe style), 39
Bering Land Bridge, 11–12
Bindings. See Army, Balata, Burgess, Heel Control, Inner tube, Nylon strap, Squaw hitch
Boots, 62–64; *ill.* 63
Burgess binding, 50–51; *ill.* 51
"Bushwhacker" (ski style), 39

Canadian Snowshoer's Union, 18, 115
Cascade-Sherpa (snowshoe style), 69
Charbonneau, Raoul, 20
Clothing. See Boots, Mittens, Moccasins, Pants, Parkas, Socks, Tuque
See also Costs, Layering principle
Clubs. See American Snowshoe Union, Canadian Snow-Shoer's Union, Montreal Snow Shoe Club
Costs, 68
Coureur de bois, 67
Crampons, 50–51, 69–70; *ill.* 51
Crust spikes, 50–51, 58; *ill.* 51

Deer, 86–87; *ill.* 86
Delia, Joe, 39, 53–55
Downhill travel techniques, 79–80; *ill.* 79

Edging, 77
Emergency
equipment, 91–93, 152–155
See also Rescue techniques, Survival techniques
Equipment. See Bindings, Boots, Clothing, Crampons, Emergency equipment, Ice axe, Poles, Snowshoes
See also Costs
Eskimos, 12

Family outings. See Outings
Felt boots, 62–64; *ill.* 63
First aid, 95–96
Footgear. See Boots
French Canadians, 13
Frostbite, 96

Games, 120–125. See also Racing
Gilman, Roger, 36, 38
Green Mountain modified bearpaw (snowshoe style), 29–30, 35, 47, 73, 133; *ill.* 30
Group travel, 85–90
Grouse, 87–88
Gut, 44. See also Babiche

Headgear. See Tuque
Heel control binding, 55–58, 69; *ill.* 57
Hill climbing technique, 75–77; *ill.* 76
Horse, snowshoes for, 36–37; *ill.* 37
Huron Indians, 16
Hypothermia, 95–96

Ice axe, 71
Ice travel technique, 84–85
Indians, 12, 16, 43; *ill.* 13, 14, 43
Inner tube (rubber) binding, 58–60; *ill.* 59, 60

Jigs, for making snowshoes, 139–141; *ill.* 140, 141

Kits, snowshoe, 152

Lacing. *See* Babiche, Neoprene, Nylon
  *See Also* Lacing patterns
Lacing patterns, 44–45, 147–152
  *See also* Lacing
Lamp wick binding, 50
Layering principle (clothing), 64
Leadership, 88–89, 91

Magnesium snowshoes, 36
Maine (snowshoe style), 31–32, 47; *ill.* 32
Making snowshoes, 126–154; *ill.* 134, 136, 137, 140, 141, 145, 146, 150, 151, 152
  *See also* Babiche, Jigs, Lacing patterns, Manufacture, commercial, Steamer, Wood for snowshoes
Manufacture, commercial, 39–45; *ill.* 41
  *See also* Making Snowshoes
Manufacturers. *See* Manufacturers List, 155
Michigan (snowshoe style), 31–32, 47, 133; *ill.* 32
Military snowshoes, 13–15, 31–32, 36, 50–52; *ill.* 15
Mittens, 66
Moccasins, 62–64; *ill.* 63
Montreal Snow Shoe Club, 18–20; *ill.* 19

Neoprene lacing, 42–43
  *See also* Babiche
Northfield, Vermont, 21
Nylon lacing, 45. *See also* Babiche
Nylon strap binding, 49–50

Ojibwa (snowshoe style), 32–33, 133, 141, 146, 150–152; *ill.* 32, 141, 145, 146, 150, 151, 152
Outings, 24–25; *ill.* 23
  *See also* Games, Racing

Pants, 64–67
Parkas, 65–66
Pickerel (snowshoe style), 33

Plastic snowshoes, 32, 34–35; *ill.* 35
Poles, 70–71, 73, 80–81; *ill.* 71, 81

Racing, on snowshoes, 17–18, 115–120; *ill.* 116, 117, 118, 119
Rawhide lacing, 44. *See also* Babiche
Reindeer hide boots, 61
Repairs, of snowshoes, 71–72, 92, 93; *ill.* 92
Rescue techniques, 107–114; *ill.* 113

Skis, 16, 39
Sleds, 112–113; *ill.* 113
Snowmobile boots, 63; *ill.* 63
Snowmobiles, 26–27, 107
Snowshoe construction, *See* Making snowshoes and Manufacture, commercial
Snowshoe selection, 28–39, 45–47; *ill.* 30, 32, 35
  *See also* Snowshoe styles
Snowshoe styles. *See* Alaskan, Algonquin, Bearpaw, Beavertail, Cascade-Sherpa, Green Mountain modified bearpaw, Maine, Michigan, Ojibwa, Pickerel, Trail, Westover
  *See also* Kits, Magnesium snowshoes, Plastic snowshoes
Snowshoeing. *See* Techniques
"Snowtreads" (snowshoe style), 34
Socks, 62, 64
Squaw hitch binding, 55–56, 67; *ill.* 56
"Steamer," for making snowshoes, 143; *ill.* 136
Survival techniques, 93–94, 108–114; *ill.* 113

Techniques. *See* Downhill travel, Edging, Group Travel, Hill climbing, Ice travel, Racing, Traversing, Turning techniques
Teslin Indians, 43
Toe hole, 46
Trail (snowshoe style), 33; *ill.* 32
Trail breaking, 82–83, 112
Traversing, 76–78; *ill.* 74, 76
"Truger" (snowshoe style), 39
Tuque, 66
Turning techniques, 77–78

Uniforms, snowshoe club, 17–18; *Ill.* 17, 19

Varnish, on snowshoes, 46, 151

Weight and size, 46–47
Westover modified bearpaw (snowshoe style), 29, 31, 47, 73

Whales (snowshoe style), 39
Whippers-In, 22, 89
Wood, for snowshoes, 129–133, 154; *ill.* 131
Wooden (board) snowshoes, 37–38; *ill.* 37, 38

The lure of the snowshoe trail.